THE FINANCIAL ADVISOR'S
ULTIMATE
STRESS MASTERY GUIDE

The Financial Advisor's ULTIMATE Stress Mastery Guide:
77 Proven Prescriptions to Build Your Resilience

Copyright © 2014 Jack Singer, PhD

All Rights Reserved.
No part of this book may be reproduced in any form or by any means, electronic or mechanical, including photocopying, recording, or by any information storage and retrieval system, without permission in writing from the author and publisher.

ISBN: 978-0-9700694-4-3

Published by

Dana Point, CA

Some tables and figures featured in this book have been replicated with permission and were developed by Dr. Jack Singer.

Edited by Mary Mihaly
Book design by Stacey Aaronson

Printed in the USA

The Financial Advisor's ULTIMATE Stress Mastery *Guide*

Proven Prescriptions
to
Build Your Resilience

Jack Singer, PhD

*I dedicate this book to Rose and Bill Singer, Selma and Leo Nadel,
Barbara Schiffman, Jamie Schiavo, and Reid Monroe,
who all left our families too soon,
and to Kensington (Kenzi) and Collins (C.K.) Piccola, our newest arrivals.*

Contents

Acknowledgements   *i*
Preface   *iii*

PART I. UNDERSTANDING THE REAL CAUSES OF YOUR STRESS

1. HOW STRESS CAN KICK THE HEALTH OUT OF YOU   1

    Learning Objectives   1
    Tales of a Saber-Toothed Tiger   8
    The Incredible Mind-Body Connection   11
       Stresses Inherent in Financial Advising   13
    Some Stress Is Actually *Good* for You   15
    Action Plan for Stress Mastery   19

2. HOW LIFE EVENTS AND CHANGES CAN IMPACT STRESS AND ILLNESS   21

    Learning Objectives   21
    Your Recent Life Changes Score and Its Interpretations   27
       Low LCU Score (0 to 199)   27
       Moderate LCU Score (200 to 299)   27
       Elevated LCU Score (300 to 449)   27
       High LCU Score (450 and higher)   28
    The Life Event Stressors Inherent in Advising   29
    Action Plan for Stress Mastery   35

3. HOW TO RECOGNIZE THE REAL CULPRIT: YOUR INTERNAL CRITIC   37

    Learning Objectives   37
    Understanding the Real Causes of Your Stress   38
    The Origins of Our Belief Systems   39
    The Young Financial Advisor's Biggest Challenge: Impostor Fear   42
    Our Self-Talk and Our Emotions   44
    Expose and Dispose of Your Internal Critic   48
    Common Negative Self-Talk Patterns   48
    Action Plan for Stress Mastery   59

4.	How to Thrive Despite Being Genetically Wired with Stress-Prone Personality Traits	**61**
	Learning Objectives	61
	Two Personality Types That Promote Stress	63
	You Can Start Modifying Some of Your Type-A Behaviors Today!	69
	How to Use Active-Listening Skills	85
	You Can Start Modifying Some of Your People-Pleasing Behaviors Today!	87
	How to Assert Yourself	88
	Action Plan for Stress Mastery	99
5.	How to Deflect Stressors: Carefully Planned Plus Warp-Speed Techniques	**101**
	Learning Objectives	101
	Recognize Your Thinking Patterns	103
	The Thinking-Pattern Worksheet (TPW)	104
	A Thought-Stopping Technique	111
	A Calming-Breathing Technique	111
	Write-It-Down Technique	112
	Worry-Time Technique	112
	Make a Contract with Yourself	113
	Action Plan for Stress Mastery	114

PART II. PRESCRIPTIONS FOR BUILDING YOUR PSYCHOLOGICAL IMMUNITY TO STRESS

6.	How to Harness the Power Within and Inoculate Yourself Against the Impact of Inevitable Stressors	**119**
	Learning Objectives	119–20
	How to Begin the Inoculation Process	120
	How to Build Resilience to Stress: The Three Cs of Stress Hardiness	121
	Commitment	121
	Control	122
	Challenge	122
	The Power of Self-Efficacy	123
	How Can You Develop a Resilient Sense of Self-Efficacy?	124
	How to Use the Power of Goal Setting to Stay Focused Despite Stress Provocations	128
	The Power of Desire, Imagination, and Expectation	130

How to Use the Power of Positive Affirmations
    to Develop the Three Cs and Accomplish Your Goals 131
        Commitment 132
        Control 132
        Challenge 133
        Goals 133
        Change 133
        Confidence 133
        Believing in Myself 134
    Action Plan for Stress Mastery 135

7. HOW TO SELECT AND RETAIN IDEAL CLIENTS **137**
    Learning Objectives 137
    Toxic Personalities to Avoid 139
    How to Eliminate Toxic People from Your Practice 144
    Stick to Your Core Values as an Advisor 145
    How to Attract Female Clients into Your Practice 147
    Why Women Become Disenchanted with Their Advisors 149
    Women's Financial Fears and Unmet Needs
        in the Financial Arena 150
    How You Can Capitalize on This Opportunity: Begin by Listening 151
        Additional Ways to Solicit and Accommodate Female Clients 154
    Action Plan for Stress Mastery 157

8. HOW TO BECOME AND REMAIN A RESILIENT PERSON **159**
    Learning Objectives 159
    Learning to Become Optimistic 161
    How to Bring More Joy and Happiness into Your Life 172
    More Behavioral Prescriptions to Build Resiliency 174
        Proven Personal Prescriptions 175
    In Closing . . . No . . . This Is Actually Your Beginning! 183
    Action Plan for Stress Mastery 186

Resources *189*
Appendix A: Glossary of Acronyms *197*
Appendix B: 77 Behavioral Prescriptions to Master Stress and
    Build Your Resilience *199*
Appendix C: A Deep-Muscle Relaxation Technique *211*
About the Author *219*

Acknowledgements

My hat goes off to all of the advisors with whom I consulted during my journey of joy while writing this book. My work with financial advisors for the past ten years has filled me with admiration and respect. In particular, I acknowledge Brian, Carl, Susan, Jay, Matt, Melanie, Tom, Deborah, Danny, Marty, David, and Karen, the advisors who graciously gave of their time and allowed me to share their secrets of success over stress.

The following advisors have given me permission to list their full names and contact information:

David L. Bahnsen, CFP, CIMA
Managing Director & Senior Portfolio Manager
The Bahnsen Group
Morgan Stanley Wealth Management
800 Newport Center Drive, Suite 700
Newport Beach, CA 92660
www.thebahnsengroup.com

Brian Boggs, President
Adviser Assets Solutions, Pty Ltd.
Suite 704, Level 7, 70 Castlereagh Street
Sydney NSW 2000, Australia
www.advisorassetssolutions.com

Karen J. Ellenbacker, President
Ellenbacker Investment Group, Inc.
N35 W23877 Highfield Court, Suite 200
Pewaukee, Wisconsin 53072
www.ellenbecker.com

Martin V. Higgins CFP, CLU, AEP
Family Wealth Management, LLC
9000 Lincoln Drive East
Suite 300A
Marlton, NJ 08053
www.familywealthadvisory.com

Securities offered through Mutual of Omaha Investor Services, Inc., a Registered Broker/Dealer. Member FINRA/SIPC. Advisory services offered through Mutual of Omaha Investor Services, Inc., an SEC Registered Investment Advisory Firm. Jack Singer, Family Wealth Management, LLC, and Mutual of Omaha Investor Services, Inc. are not affiliated.

Danny Smith, President
Daniels Financial Group, Inc.
5505 Detroit Rd., Suite A
Sheffield Village, OH 44054
www.danielsfinancialgroup.com

Securities offered through Mutual of Omaha Investor Services, Inc., a Registered Broker/Dealer. Member FINRA/SIPC. Advisory services offered through Mutual of Omaha Investor Services, Inc., an SEC Registered Investment Advisory Firm. Jack Singer, Daniels Financial Group, Inc., and Mutual of Omaha Investor Services, Inc. are not affiliated.

Jay Van Beusekom, Financial Advisor, LLC
W Park Pl, Ste 980
Milwaukee, WI 53224
www.why-jay.com

Securities offered through Mutual of Omaha Investor Services, Inc., a Registered Broker/Dealer. Member FINRA/SIPC. Advisory services offered through Mutual of Omaha Investor Services, Inc., an SEC Registered Investment Advisory Firm. Jack Singer, Jay Van Beusekom Financial Advisor, LLC, and Mutual of Omaha Investor Services, Inc. are not affiliated.

Thanks to Corwin Publishers and Editor Arnis Burvikovs for giving me permission to use sections of my earlier book, *The Teacher's Ultimate Stress Mastery Guide*.

Preface

Knowledge without action is the greatest self-con of all.
—Sharon Wegscheider Cruse, author

A major study of the emotional well-being of financial advisors during the 2008 financial crisis (Fairchild, 2013), showed that 93 percent of the advisors surveyed reported medium to high stress levels, and 39 percent reported stress symptoms at levels compatible with Post-Traumatic Stress Disorder (PTSD).

When we think about PTSD, we typically envision tornadoes, hurricanes, combat, and other life-threatening events. But PTSD is not limited to such huge catastrophes. Events threatening financial security and even a threat to one's career can be terribly traumatic as well.

For advisors, the financial crisis was not only a perceived threat to the security of their careers, but a threat to their own portfolios. After all, in an ideal world, advisors basically make the same financial decisions and use the same strategies with regard to their own portfolios, as they would make for their clients'. As such, many advisors suffered the double whammy of major losses in both their clients' portfolios and their own. Added to this stress was getting bombarded with calls from frightened, disgruntled, and hostile clients, blaming the advisor for not having seen this crisis coming.

A study reported by Rhode (2013) examined the risk of PTSD associated with sudden and dramatic personal financial loss. The authors surveyed 173 Madoff victims and found that 58 percent met the criteria for the PTSD diagnosis, 61 percent acknowledged high levels of anxiety, 58 percent were depressed, and 34 percent had health-related issues. Moreover, 90 percent of these victims felt a substantial loss of confidence in any financial institutions. In short, severe economic trauma can certainly lead to PTSD, and you can imagine the traumatic and stressful repercussions from these clients to their advisors.

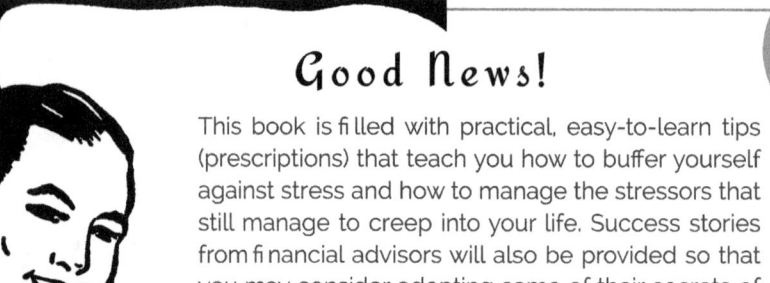

Good News!

This book is filled with practical, easy-to-learn tips (prescriptions) that teach you how to buffer yourself against stress and how to manage the stressors that still manage to creep into your life. Success stories from financial advisors will also be provided so that you may consider adopting some of their secrets of success for dealing with your own stress.

It doesn't take the trauma of a financial or economic crisis or "trusted" advisors perpetrating Ponzi schemes to dramatically raise the stress levels of advisors. Citing the "lack of available research conducted with stockbrokers," Dr. Alden Cass and his associates (2000) embarked on a landmark study of Wall Street stockbrokers, all male, with an average age of 26. Among his findings was the fact that these stockbrokers were suffering from major symptoms of job burnout, anxiety, and depression. In fact, nearly a quarter of the participants met the criteria for a clinical diagnosis of major depression, while the National Institute of Mental Health (2000) reported that same year that the diagnosis of major depression for all men in the U.S. was only seven percent. This finding of disproportionate stress-related outcomes for stockbrokers stimulated Alden Class and his associates (2008) to write an important book to help financial professionals cope with inevitable and unpredictable stressors connected with their jobs.

ONGOING JOB STRESSORS FOR ADVISORS

The role of the financial advisor is filled with everyday, potential stressors, including:

- $ Wearing multiple "hats," including psychologist, social worker, seminar producer, marketing manager, confidante, time manager, fiduciary and compliance expert, trust attorney, research analyst, referral prospector, and CPA
- $ Dealing with demanding, PITA (pain in the ___) clients
- $ Conflicting demands from managers and clients
- $ Competition
- $ Establishing a trusted team
- $ Maintaining professional development (continuing education)
- $ Balancing work, family, recreation, and relaxation

MY BURGEONING INTEREST IN WORKING WITH FINANCIAL ADVISORS

Over my 30-plus years as a clinical psychologist, I have treated many advisors suffering from a variety of stress-related emotional symptoms, including fear of failure, anxiety, depression, anger, and burnout. In my role as a sport psychologist, I have seen many advisors who were "weekend warriors," using their sport as a vehicle for expressing their pent-up aggression and frustration.

Then, in 2011, Brian Boggs, past president of the New South Wales Australia Financial Advisors' Association, contacted me after reading some articles I had published on stress causes and stress mastery. Brian informed me that the governments of Australia and New Zealand had recently imposed fee-for-service demands on advisors, removing the traditional commission-based services. This change led to a large percentage of advisors panicking and contemplating seeking new careers. Many advisors began to question whether they could continue to work in a profession where they had the huge fiduciary responsibility of safeguarding their clients' family savings; moreover, making midlife career changes was also traumatic, so many advisors facing these decisions felt trapped.

As a result of those concerns, Brian and I developed an audio stress-mastery program, specifically for advisors, and my career as a psychologist began to focus in large part on helping people in the financial advising profession. This spawned the idea to produce a stress mastery guide for advisors, featuring all of the cutting-edge research in the field and applying it specifically to that audience.

This guide is intended to be a "rat-eared," self-help primer that you revisit often to find precise prescriptions not only for mastering the stressors in your job and life, but also for reminders of how you can be proactive and greatly reduce your vulnerability to those stressors. Ideally, you will learn how to *prevent* the symptoms of distress and burnout. In essence, you will develop a Teflon-like resilience to the stressors that will inevitably cross your path.

The behavioral prescriptions contained in this guide are all based on state-of-the-art research in the fields of Cognitive Behavioral Therapy, Stress Mastery, Resilience Theory, and the New Positive Psychology for Authentic Happiness.

In addition to the comments of nationally recognized advisors I have interviewed, much of my information is based on the many advisor clients I have treated over the past 33 years in my private and consulting practices. The goals here are to rivet your attention to the nuts and bolts of mastering stress and preventing burnout with easy-to-learn, proven strategies that *really work!*

Each chapter begins with a list of learning objectives and focuses on a real-life anecdote about one or more financial advisors.

You'll also find special features throughout the book, including "Good News" boxes, which direct you to practical actions that can lower your stress level, and "Stress Mastery Prescriptions"—tools to help you take charge of your emotional well-being, in both the short and the long term. Finally, each chapter concludes with a specific Action Plan, which summarizes what you learned in the chapter and includes a checklist to help you integrate your new behavioral skills into your everyday repertoire. You'll see several blank boxes in each Action Plan where you can include additional behaviors and skills you began to practice as a result of reading that chapter. So keep this book close by and relax, knowing there is an Action Plan available at the end of each chapter to keep you on target.

It is important to realize that you don't have to be perfect and master all 77 prescriptions in order to make a major improvement in your life. All of the Stress Mastery Prescriptions are listed together in Appendix B for easy review, so you can pick and choose prescriptions as the need presents.

Although learning the exact sources of your stress and how to become more resilient to them is the basic purpose of this book, *practicing* your new skills is essential to success. With practice, you will succeed in developing new habits, which will help you insulate or *inoculate* yourself against the devastations of psychological burnout.

Have a highlighter and pen handy. Mark or put asterisks next to the sections, descriptions, advisor stories, phrases, and Action Plans that affect your life, and which you will want to find easily for review. Consider using a red pen to mark passages that give you hope, and write "Good News" in the margin.

Actually, there are many more than 77 proven behavioral prescriptions included to help you succeed, as several contain multiple suggestions and many of the tables have additional prescriptions. My goal is for this book to be a comfort to you, helping you to realize there are behaviors you can put into action immediately to overcome any issue or problem in your financial advising career.

If you skip around, be sure to go back and read the sections you skipped because there are prescriptions scattered throughout each chapter, which you may want to put to use immediately. Choose new prescriptions to incorporate into your weekly routine and practice, practice, practice. Research shows that if you utilize these skills consistently, you should see positive changes in about 21 days (Fishel, 2003).

Besides personal skills, the prescriptions also include suggestions to bring to your office and to share with your colleagues. Because stress in the financial advising profession is so pervasive, consider organizing an advisor support group in your community. This way, all members can share ideas and learn what their colleagues have successfully done in their practices and lives to overcome their stress.

Although we are all victims of unfortunate, self-defeating, habitual patterns of setting ourselves up for distress and letting it get the best of us, we are certainly capable of breaking through the psychological shackles that have bound us since we were children, to explore new ways of thinking and reacting that are positive and beneficial. For many of us embracing change is risky, but those risks certainly have their rewards. You have many choices in life; among them is choosing to change unfortunate beliefs, assumptions, and behaviors that have kept you trapped in a cocoon of unhappiness, stress, and despair. For many of you, choosing to make changes represents risk; however, most well-thought-out risks reap lifetime rewards. Robert Frost said it best:

Two roads diverged in a wood, and I—I took the one less traveled by,
And that has made all the difference.

—From *The Road Not Taken and Other Poems,* by Robert Frost, p. 1,
Dover Publications, Stanley Applebaum, Editor, 1993. Used with permission.

NOTE: The Resources section in the back of the book provides a list of references used in building each chapter.

Enjoy this journey to health, success, and happiness.
In many ways, your life depends on it.

PART I

UNDERSTANDING *the* REAL CAUSES *of* YOUR STRESS

1

How Stress Can Kick *the* Health Out *of* You

A critical shift in medicine has been the recognition that many of the damaging diseases of slow accumulation can be either caused or made far worse by stress.

—Robert Sapolsky (1998)

LEARNING OBJECTIVES

- I will be able to recognize the potential impact on my health from long-term stressors.
- I will understand the powerful mind and body connection.
- I will know how to calm myself quickly whenever I am feeling stressed.
- I will be able to cite the specific stressors at work and in my life that affect me on a regular basis.
- I will understand the concept of eustress and how some stress actually helps me to be successful in life.

Growing up in near-poverty, Brian was forced to drop out of high school and never had an opportunity to go to college. Living in New Zealand, he envisioned a life of average means because of his lack of higher education. Upon moving to Australia after the birth of his first child and concerned about being able to provide for his family, he took a leap of faith by taking courses and obtaining the required education and licenses to become a financial planner. He soon discovered that he could really help his clients, and this optimistic attitude resulted in a very comfortable income.

The lifestyle Brian was developing required complete devotion to his job—to the detriment of his family—but it was hard to slow down with the money pouring in. Brian had a multitude of stressors impacting him, and they generated a host of symptoms, including:

- $ Feeling emotionally overworked (burning the candle at both ends) and drained by the time he got home each day
- $ Getting out of bed exhausted each morning and feeling like he was heading off to a battle
- $ Rarely delegating responsibilities, contributing to the overwork that was making him ill
- $ Demanding perfection and being impatient with anyone who wouldn't comply
- $ Micromanaging everything and yelling at employees and product provider staff
- $ Giving himself little or no time for exercise
- $ Eating an unhealthy diet
- $ Feeling paranoid about making any mistakes with his clients' money
- $ Trying to placate his highest value client, who was a real bully toward both Brian and his employees

Yet, despite the stressors in his life, Brian was at the top of his game. His business was awarded the title of "Australian Advice Practice of the Year" and following that, he received the prestigious "Advisor of the Year" award. His income grew to more than a million dollars annually.

It was then that Brian's stress "kicked the health out of him." He was diagnosed with an aggressive cancer that required immediate surgery, which Brian attributed directly to his stressors. You'll see the happy conclusion of Brian's story at the end of this chapter.

On June 6, 1983, "Stress!" was on the cover of *Time* Magazine, and it was referred to as the "epidemic of the eighties" and the nation's primary health problem (American Institute of Stress [AIS], n.d.). Job stress was listed as, by far, the leading source of stress among Americans.

More than two decades later, Americans were still stressed out. On December 12, 2007, results from the American Psychological Association's (APA) annual survey of stress among the general public in the United States was released (APA, 2007). This "Stress in America" survey listed results from close to 2000 Americans, 18 and older, and the survey was conducted in both English and Spanish.

Most of those surveyed (79 percent) said that they could not avoid stress in their lives. A total of 77 percent of those surveyed experienced stress-related physical symptoms, including headaches, gastrointestinal (GI) problems, and unexplained fatigue. Nearly half of those surveyed (43 percent) blamed problems with their families or personal time on their stress levels (APA, 2007).

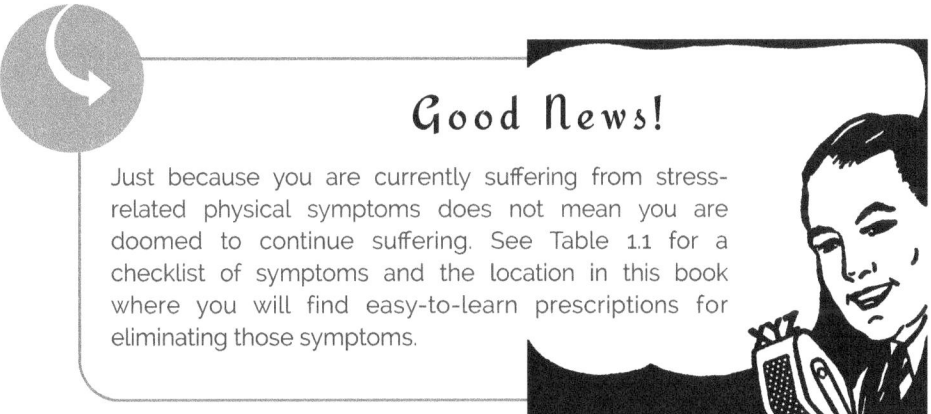

Good News!

Just because you are currently suffering from stress-related physical symptoms does not mean you are doomed to continue suffering. See Table 1.1 for a checklist of symptoms and the location in this book where you will find easy-to-learn prescriptions for eliminating those symptoms.

The survey was repeated in September 2008, with data gathered between June and August 2008 (APA, 2008). Nearly half (47 percent) of respondents reported increases in their stress levels since 2007. In the report, Dr. Katherine Nadal, APA's executive director for professional practice, said: "People's emotional and physical health is more vulnerable, given the high levels of stress in our country right now" (APA, 2008).

You can see from the prescriptions side of Table 1.1 that this book is filled with plenty of easy-to-learn remedies and buffers to help you ward off stressors and eradicate them once they are in place.

Notice that your stress-related symptoms are broken down into five categories:

- 💲 anxiety
- 💲 depression
- 💲 physical
- 💲 behavior
- 💲 relationship symptoms

Most people have a combination of symptoms across all of these categories, and many studies show that folks with chronic anxiety or depressive symptoms, combined with hostility and cynicism, have double the risk of developing the diseases and symptoms listed under physical symptoms.

Table 1.1 — CHECKLIST OF POTENTIAL STRESS SYMPTOMS AND SELF-HELP PRESCRIPTIONS THAT REALLY WORK

Copy this table and check all of the symptoms that apply to you. Add any additional ones you are experiencing. Note the chapters and resources where prescriptions to resolve those symptoms are discussed and visit Appendix B to find additional prescriptions that also address these symptoms.

Anxiety Symptoms	Prescriptions
☐ Desperate	*Recognize your Life Event Changes* (see Chapter 2)
☐ Feeling as if you are losing control	
☐ Frightened	*Take charge of future life events* (see Chapter 2)
☐ Irritable and frustrated	
☐ Negative, self-defeating thinking	*Relax your muscles* (see Appendix C)
☐ Nervous, on edge, uptight	*Recognize your distorted thoughts* (see Chapter 3)
☐ Panicky	
☐ Racing thoughts	*Use the Thinking-Pattern Worksheet (TPW)* (see Chapter 5)
☐ Sense of impending doom	
☐ Worrying	*Realize that these symptoms are temporary, and they will lift once you take charge of your thinking and planning for the future* (see Chapter 8)
☐	
☐	
☐	

Depression Symptoms	Prescriptions
☐ Appetite changes ☐ Concentration difficulties ☐ Helplessness ☐ Hopelessness ☐ Indecisiveness ☐ Isolation and avoiding contacts ☐ Loss of confidence ☐ Loss of energy ☐ Loss of interests ☐ Loss of motivation ☐ Loss of sex drive ☐ Poor self-esteem ☐ Sadness ☐ Sleeping changes ☐ Suicidal thoughts ☐ ☐ ☐	*Recognize your distorted thoughts* *(see Chapter 3)* *Use the TPW* *(see Chapter 5)* *Use the Thought-Stopping Technique* *(see Chapter 5)* *Practice relaxation techniques* *(see Appendix C)* *Be more assertive* *(see Chapter 4)*

| Table 1.1 | (CONTINUED) |

Physical Symptoms	Prescriptions
☐ Agitation ☐ Chest and/or muscle tightness ☐ Diarrhea or constipation ☐ Feeling dizzy or lightheaded ☐ Feeling tired and weak ☐ Headaches, migraine, and tension ☐ Muscle tightness, pain, and spasms ☐ Racing heart ☐ Restlessness or jumpiness **Reduced disease immunity may lead to or inflame a host of diseases, including:** ☐ Asthma ☐ Back and neck pain ☐ Cancer ☐ Cardiovascular disorders, including high blood pressure and chest pain ☐ Dermatological disorders ☐ Diabetes ☐ Gastrointestinal disorders ☐ Headaches ☐ ☐ ☐	*Practice relaxation techniques (see Appendix C)* *Practice assertiveness skills (see Chapter 4)* *Practice stress hardiness (see Chapter 6)*

Behavior Symptoms	Prescriptions
☐ Anger and hostility ☐ Harmful habits (overeating, use of substances, smoking, gambling, overspending) ☐ Impatience ☐ Impulsivity ☐ Irritability ☐ Rapid speech ☐ Resentment ☐ Procrastination ☐ Withdrawal ☐ ☐ ☐	℞ *Practice relaxation techniques (see Appendix C)* ℞ *Practice assertiveness skills (see Chapter 4)* ℞ *Practice stress hardiness skills (see Chapter 6)*
Relationship Symptoms	*Prescriptions*
☐ Intimacy issues ☐ Lack of assertiveness ☐ Not listening to partner's needs ☐ Short fuse with partner or friends ☐ Parenting disagreements ☐ Poor communications ☐ Power struggles ☐ ☐ ☐	℞ *Practice active-listening skills (see Chapters 4 and 7)* ℞ *Practice assertiveness skills (see Chapter 4)*

℞ № 1

Take care of your emotional health by taking care of your physical health. Consider visiting a licensed naturopathic physician to learn about foods and natural supplements that have been proven to reduce and prevent stress. The following are examples of healthy habits that have been shown to directly impact moods and stress levels:

* Keep your blood sugar low with frequent, smaller meals that include protein.
* Eat light at night.
* Get ample sleep.
* Avoid alcohol, caffeine, and tobacco.
* Load up on antioxidant-rich foods.
* Keep your weight in the normal range for your age and height.

♦ ♦ ♦

There are also potential emotional warning signs of stress-related burnout that are common among financial advisors, including the following:

- $ difficulty sleeping well on Sunday evenings
- $ avoiding work and calling in sick
- $ having difficulty concentrating on tasks
- $ feeling overwhelmed by the workload
- $ forgetting appointments

TALES OF A SABER-TOOTHED TIGER

A large body of evidence suggests that stress-related disease emerges, predominantly, out of the fact that we so often activate a physiological system that has evolved for responding to acute physical emergencies, but we turn it on for months on end, worrying about mortgages, relationships and promotions.

—Robert Sapolsky (1998)

Hans Seyle, a Canadian physician and researcher, known as the "Father of Stress," defined stress as "the nonspecific response of the body to any demand." So stress is the feeling we get in response to any stressor (Seyle, 1976), whether it takes place at work or at home. Stressors—such as injury, illness, or pain—throw your body out of balance. The stress response is part of your body's automatic attempt to restore balance, referred to as homeostasis. But it is critical to understand that for humans stressors also include beliefs, fears, worries, anticipation of something bad happening, and anything in our thinking that provokes the stress response. As you will learn throughout this book, these stressors are strictly under our control, and we can eliminate them once we understand them.

Of course, our bodies have been hot-wired genetically to deal with stressors involved in physical danger as a matter of survival. Visualize a caveman (or woman) coming out of the cave one morning, stretching and contemplating the day's tasks. As our friend looks around, he spots a hungry saber-toothed tiger 20 yards away. This recognition of a serious danger throws the brain into emergency mode through the sympathetic nervous system (SNS), genetically programmed to prepare him for the fight, flight, or freeze response to this stressor. The SNS is so named because it provides a sympathy link between our perceptions and thoughts and the feelings in our internal organs.

Once he sees the tiger and thinks about the danger, the caveman's SNS automatically turns on several systems in his body, which begin the process of adapting to and dealing with this potentially life-threatening stressor. The resultant stress response includes the following actions:

- $ Blood that would be completing the digestive process moves away from the GI system to the external muscles. During this emergency stress response, there is no time for the slow process of digestion; plus, this would require energy that would better serve the muscles for reacting in the fight, flight, or freeze response to the stressor.

- $ Perspiration increases to cool the body, which helps it burn more energy for fight, flight, or freeze responses.

- $ Muscles, particularly in the arms, legs, back, and neck, tighten to be ready to act quickly.

- $ Glucose pours into the bloodstream to provide instant energy for the fight, flight, or freeze reaction to this stressor.

- $ His heart rate, blood pressure, and respiratory rate all increase to transport nutrients and oxygen at greater rates to his brain to help him make decisions, and to his muscles to prepare for action.

- $ Adrenalin from the adrenal glands pours into the bloodstream to keep him alert.

- $ Cortisol, known as the stress hormone, is released to increase energy and strengthen the body's defenses.

- $ Blood clotting chemicals spring to action in the bloodstream to prevent excess bleeding in case there is an injury that takes place during the fight, flight, or freeze response.
- $ The immune system is inhibited. This is fine for the short term, when you don't need it to be making antibodies to protect you from viruses and diseases that may threaten your health or life months down the road. However, this is a critical reaction because the long-term inhibition of the immune system from continual exposure to stressors (and continually switching on the SNS) suppresses the immune function and strips the body of its natural protection from diseases.

You can appreciate the remarkable adaptation of the human body through evolution to deal with obvious life-threatening and dangerous emergencies, but because these emergencies were infrequent when man first existed, the system was designed to switch on infrequently. Grazing animals, for example, have to switch on this nervous system periodically when they are threatened by predators, but the encounter is usually relatively short lived, and the animal then relaxes and goes about its business of grazing.

For humans, the SNS also responds to situations and events that we interpret and think about—typically not emergencies or threats. Unfortunately, our brain does not recognize the difference between a real threat and one that we anticipate by vividly imagining something awful or sad happening to us in the future.

For example, if I ask you to use all of your senses to visualize yourself biting into a juicy lemon right now, you will begin to salivate automatically and your glands secrete a base solution into your mouth (saliva) to counteract the acid from the lemon. So the brain takes its directions from your thoughts and images, even though what you are visualizing and thinking about is not actually occurring.

Think about what may be a typical day for you: You had a rough day at the office, with several of your clients phoning you, complaining about how the market has affected their portfolios. One of those clients is insisting that you meet with her today. Moreover, you got word from your non-supportive manager that because of budget cuts, your favorite assistant's position will be eliminated by the end of the week. You said the following to yourself:

I'm having enough trouble trying to find the time to research new investment products for my clients without these disruptions and challenges. My clients will never understand how to build their portfolios if I can't get the necessary research completed. Once my favorite assistant leaves, my workload will be unmanageable. I'm in no mood to deal with this angry client today. My boss never supports me. This isn't fair. I don't know what to do.

Each of these anxiety-producing thoughts, beliefs, and predictions represents a psychological stressor that has evolved relatively recently in our evolutionary development. Each is a potential upset to our internal system, switching on the SNS the same way that a real emergency does.

THE INCREDIBLE MIND-BODY CONNECTION

> *The evidence is growing stronger that states of mind can affect physical health.*
> —Goleman and Gurin (1993)

As I mentioned, our brains do not differentiate real dangers from those we craft in our minds when we worry about actual or anticipated disturbing events in our lives. Each physiological response to life-threatening stressors serves a critical, life-preserving purpose, as noted in the earlier examples; but because our bodies were designed only to activate this SNS infrequently and when our lives are actually in danger, the daily switching on that so many of us experience because of our worrying puts tremendous strain on the system. The result is the potential for physiological damage. Therefore, as scientists Robert Sapolsky (1998) and Hans Seyle (1976) describe, each adaptive response has a debilitating consequence for the human body when it is triggered frequently by worries and concerns:

- Blood continually leaving the GI tract to flow into the muscles of the legs and arms preparing for the fight, flight, or freeze reaction can lead to vomiting, energy loss, and chronic digestive problems, including gastritis and irritable bowel syndrome.

- People who are constantly under stress frequently have embarrassing perspiration issues, including dampness when shaking hands.

- Muscles continually tightening up can lead to muscle spasms, tension, and pain, particularly in the neck and back. In addition, chronic muscle tension contributes to migraine and tension headaches, jaw clenching, and fatigue.

- Glucose spilling into the bloodstream often contributes to diabetes and other endocrine disorders.

- If your blood pressure rises to 180/130 when you're facing someone who is threatening your life, your body is reacting appropriately, but if your pressure is 180/130 several mornings a week as you get ready to go to work, you are at great risk for chronic cardiovascular problems and hypertension (high blood pressure), causing potential consequences such as circulation problems or heart and kidney damage. Chronic hypertension also causes feelings of nervousness and pressure.

- $ The chronic worrier or anxious person triggers the brain to spill adrenalin continuously into the bloodstream. Because a function of adrenalin is to keep you alert, a side effect of having too much adrenalin residing in your bloodstream is insomnia. This is why so many highly stressed people have sleeping difficulties.

- $ Although cortisol is necessary to prepare the muscles for vigorous reactions in the face of danger, the continual release of cortisol into the bloodstream blocks the removal of certain acids and breaks down lean tissue to convert to sugar for energy in the survival scenario. This causes ulcerations in the lining of the stomach, which is why so many people diagnosed with ulcers are people suffering from chronic stress. Long-term, chronic release of stress hormones like cortisol damages the body in many ways and leads to various diseases.

- $ Frequent blood clotting puts a person at a great risk for stroke or heart attack.

- $ Suppressing your immune functioning because of the constant switching on of the SNS can lead to disastrous consequences in terms of fighting infections and protecting you from immune system disorders, including allergies, arthritis, AIDS, lupus, some cancers, the common cold, and the flu.

We can look at any major system in the body and find evidence of symptoms being caused in whole or in part by too much activation of the stress-response system, rather than by the invasion of disease-causing bacteria or cancers. As Sapolsky (1998) explains it: "If you repeatedly turn on the stress response, or if you cannot appropriately turn off the stress response at the end of a stressful event, the stress response can eventually become nearly as damaging as some stressors themselves" (p. 16).

As you would expect, much research has linked stress with many chronic diseases and with many of the leading causes of death, including heart disease, cancer, stroke, lung diseases, and of course, suicide (Sapolsky, 1998).

Stress also affects cholesterol levels and platelet activation (causing heart attacks), and often shortens life span. Mental stressors, such as loneliness, depression, and isolation are also associated with serious illnesses and shortened life span. Sleep disorders also negatively affect the immune system and life span, and because stress is one of the main causes of the inability to fall and stay asleep, you can see the tremendous impact of stress on our overall health and longevity.

PHYSIOLOGICAL SYMPTOMS ASSOCIATED WITH STRESSES INHERENT IN FINANCIAL ADVISING

In their book *Bullish Thinking* (2008) and their report Casualties of Wall Street (2010), Cass et al cite many studies showing a clear relationship between the stressors inherent in advising and physiological symptoms. The prevalence of stress-related symptoms for advisors included:

- $ emotional exhaustion
- $ feelings of depersonalization
- $ anxiety and depression
- $ excessive alcohol and substance use
- $ burnout symptoms
- $ symptoms of Post Traumatic Stress Disorder (PTSD)

It is important to understand that the stressors we face are not actually provoked by the events that take place in our daily lives but how we interpret and think about those events—or rather, what we say to ourselves about those events. We can set off our emergency response by simply thinking about these events or anticipating potential problems befalling us in the future. Consider your stress when your manager tells you that because of your marginal performance in developing a book of business, you'll be placed on probation for one month, during which time he will determine whether you will be retained. Will you be worried about the outcome of this probationary period, even though it is a month away? Simply anticipating a problem can trigger the SNS to switch on.

A variety of sources, including the American Institute of Stress (n.d.), estimate that 75 to 90 percent of the patients who arrive at the family practice or internist's office are suffering from stress-related physical symptoms.

This is no surprise. Just look at common phrases in our everyday language: "I'm worried sick." "My job is a pain in the neck." "Sometimes I can't stomach some of my clients."

Perhaps you are aware that every drug company uses placebos (fake pills) in their research on real drugs. The companies need to prove that their drug has major effects beyond those produced in the minds of the patients who believe they are being given a drug to treat their symptoms. Hundreds of studies have determined that the optimistic, positive attitudes patients exhibit when their doctor prescribes something that "should really help you" (even though it was a benign sugar pill) lead to symptom reduction (Sapolsky, 1998; Seligman, 1998). Examples of conditions treated effectively with placebos are allergies, depression, migraine headaches, and alcohol dependence.

Besides the diseases and disorders listed previously that are caused or made worse by the impact of chronic stress, people often get themselves into more trouble when they try to cope with their stress: alcoholism, substance abuse, and chronic smoking are common coping methods people use to modify their stress. Psychotropic medications, such as antidepressants and tranquilizers, are being prescribed in record numbers. You have much more control over your physical health than you realize. Research shows that more than half of the people hospitalized in the United States could have prevented their symptoms by changing their lifestyles (Charlesworth & Nathan, 1984).

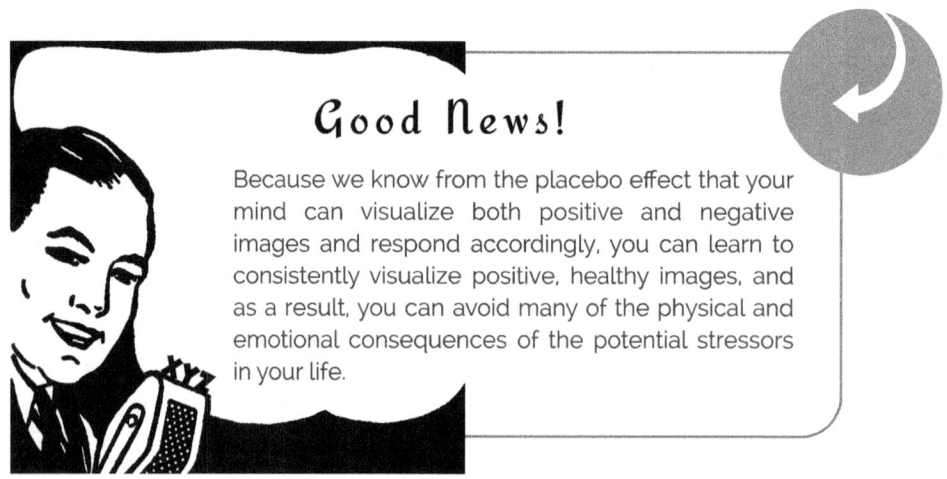

Good News!

Because we know from the placebo effect that your mind can visualize both positive and negative images and respond accordingly, you can learn to consistently visualize positive, healthy images, and as a result, you can avoid many of the physical and emotional consequences of the potential stressors in your life.

Phew! Let's all take a deep breath here ... literally—take a nice deep breath here—that alone will begin to calm you. Yes, I know ... the statistics you just reviewed are frightening, but whatever your stress level, you are not hopelessly destined to get sick or die from the stressors in your life. Although exposure to chronic or repeated stressors can potentially make you ill or increase your risk of getting a disease, such exposure does not automatically lead to illness. Many advisors under the same stress as you do not get sick. How can that be? Can we learn how to increase the effectiveness of how we cope with the stressors that surround us? We will examine these questions as we go along.

What we do know is that suffering from stress does increase your risk of getting physically sick, and if you already have a disease, stress increases the probability of your defenses collapsing, thus setting off more symptoms. But you ultimately have control over how you will internalize your thoughts and beliefs about these stressors, and those thoughts and beliefs are the keys to mastering stress.

℞ № 2

Practice breathing through your diaphragm. Put your hands on your stomach and breathe deeply in through your nose and exhale through your mouth, so that your hands move out when you inhale and move back in when you exhale. If your hands are not moving and only your shoulders and chest move when you breathe deeply, you are engaging in shallow, less relaxing breathing. You can easily teach yourself to breathe through your diaphragm with practice.

SOME STRESS IS ACTUALLY GOOD FOR YOU

> *People are not disturbed by things, but by their perception of things.*
> —EPICTETUS, GREEK PHILOSOPHER

We know that too much chronic stress can actually kill you, but did you know that too little stress is also bad for you? Hans Seyle (1976) differentiated two kinds of stress: distress and eustress. Distress is obviously the harmful, unpleasant stress, and eustress is good stress, from exciting events, job promotions, gaining a new high-value client, and so on.

Although the body reacts to eustress in exactly the same way it does to distress, eustress causes much less damage. Why? Because it's never the stressor that's the problem; rather, it's how you interpret it and what you say to yourself about that stressor that determines whether the resultant stress experience is good or bad.

Even if you have many eustress experiences in your life, such as purchasing a new home, getting married, the birth of a baby, and taking a vacation, if you worry that these events will change your life in a negative way, the resultant stress will be felt as distress. For example, you are excited about the upcoming birth of a child but incessantly worry about how you will balance taking care of a newborn in your already hectic life.

Too little stress leaves most people bored and tired. It takes a certain amount of stress to keep alert, stay motivated, think creatively, solve problems, and keep your self-confidence high. In addition, gross motor skills and reaction time work best with a manageable level of stress. Think about the times you were so relaxed that you just couldn't muster the energy to go to the gym or even do a crossword puzzle. Too little stress cuts into your motivation and productivity, but too much stress cuts into your motivation, productivity, and *health*.

℞ № 3

Recognize that you can live with a certain amount of stress in your life and that it may even be beneficial to you.

The best balance is achieved by managing the way you deal with each stressor that comes along, rather than trying to eliminate each from your life altogether—a feat you most likely cannot accomplish anyway. As an example, embracing the change that comes with having to learn about a new fiduciary responsibility that has just been mandated is actually a good thing, because you want to protect your clients in every way possible. So, rather than finding reasons to debate the new fiduciary responsibility because you fear change and are imagining how much more work is involved for you to adapt to the changes, you embrace it and move on.

℞ № 4

Ask yourself what calm people do to maintain their stress levels. Examples of answers to that question are jogging or walking each morning before work, making time for lunch each day with a calm friend or colleague, and reading articles or the rest of this book on how to master the stresses in life.

Using Table 1.2, you can check off specific coping skills you would like to learn using this book. Each of these skills is also directed at helping you to ward off stress and eradicate the stress you currently find yourself under.

Table 1.2	CHECKLIST OF ADVISOR COPING AND BUFFER SKILLS

Copy this table and check off each skill as you accomplish it. These are discussed in detail throughout the book.

Coping and Buffer Skills I Need to Work On

- ☐ Develop a strong sense of self-esteem and feel good about myself in general
- ☐ Be able to quickly determine when I am under stress (e.g., the symptoms may be hidden in frequent illnesses, vague pains, increased intake of alcohol or cigarettes, unusual weight gain or loss, or impulsive behaviors)
- ☐ Understand when I need to delay making changes in my life
- ☐ Recognize when my thinking is negative and/or distorted
- ☐ Have a series of relaxation exercises built into my week
- ☐ Take relaxing time for myself each week
- ☐ Understand if I have personality traits that make me vulnerable to stress and practice modifying those traits
- ☐ Remain optimistic regardless of circumstances
- ☐ Develop psychological hardiness skills to ward off stress
- ☐ Make sure I find funny things to laugh at each week
- ☐ Assert myself and use good listening and communication skills
- ☐ Set realistic goals for myself
- ☐ Practice acts of forgiveness, volunteerism, and help a stranger in line or in traffic
- ☐ Have exercise and healthy diet habits
- ☐ Have a gratifying visit with someone who is special in my life

Remember Brian, our workaholic advisor and cancer victim? Fortunately, just prior to his cancer diagnosis, he put together a wonderful business team and had just completed a bottom-up restructure of the entire business, overhauling all processes and procedures. Brian had decided he would actually "risk" delegating responsibilities to free up some time for himself and his family.

Brian's treatment required three months—an unplanned but remarkable learning experience. Indeed, Brian realized that the business could survive without his being constantly present. He also had plenty of time to contemplate, meditate, and reflect about his lifestyle leading up to the cancer diagnosis.

> *"I realized that my work/life balance was unbalanced; I had become a slave to building the business … and I neglected good quality home time and time for me, and even neglected my health."*

When he returned to work, Brian was sensitive to those same issues with his employees and he put into place some radical changes. For example, he rewarded employees not only with financial incentives, but also gave them the incentive of free quality time in the form of paid days off. For himself, he took every Wednesday off and went sailing, and he dramatically lightened his workload. Most importantly, he avoided stressful situations. One way he was able to do this was by selling down 80 percent of his clients and focusing on the remaining 20 percent. In addition, he designed a retirement plan (with built-in goals) so that he could accumulate enough wealth in the next seven years to retire at the age of 55, which he did.

Not only did Brian's health rebound, but people close to him told him he had become a much nicer person. And, it is really important to note that despite these dramatic changes, Brian's income continued to flourish!

In subsequent chapters, you will learn how to manage, interpret, and talk to yourself about the stressors in your life so that you can truly control your stress level.

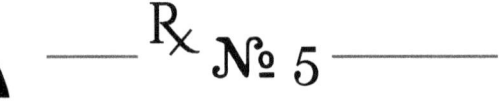

Stay fit. Run, bike, swim, walk, or hike each week. Aerobic (heart rate increasing) exercise releases endorphins—chemicals that reduce stress. Other ways to benefit from exercise are dancing, gardening, or raking leaves. You don't have to engage in vigorous activity to benefit.

♦ ♦ ♦

As was noted in the Preface, each chapter in this book will conclude with an Action Plan, which will tie back to the learning objectives for stress mastery for that chapter. Having a checklist Action Plan will help you to stay on track for practicing your new stress mastery skills.

ACTION PLAN FOR STRESS MASTERY

| Table 1.3 | MY ACTION PLAN FOR STRESS MASTERY |

Check each one when you've accomplished it. Feel free to add additional new behaviors in the spaces provided.

New Behavior	What I Did and the Date Accomplished
☐ Whenever I am feeling stressed or overwhelmed, I will calm myself by taking a series of slow, deep breaths in through my nose and out through my mouth. ☐ ☐ ☐	What I did: Date accomplished:
☐ I will not get overwhelmed by worrying about stress. I will tell myself that I can live with some stress and actually use it to my benefit. ☐ ☐ ☐	What I did: Date accomplished:
☐ I will embrace change, rather than resist it, and look for ways that change will lead to positive outcomes. ☐ ☐ ☐	What I did: Date accomplished:

(Continued)

| Table 1.3 | MY ACTION PLAN FOR STRESS MASTERY (CONT.) |

New Behavior	What I Did and the Date Accomplished
☐ I will list all of the stressors related to my job that are currently affecting me, and then I will find something positive to say about as many of these stressors as possible. ☐ ☐ ☐	What I did:
	Date accomplished:
☐ I will list positive stressors in my life that actually help me (eustress). ☐ ☐ ☐	What I did:
	Date accomplished:

2

How Life Events *and* Changes Can Impact Stress *and* Illness

As individuals, we have different needs and differing abilities to adjust to life. However, if we want a greater share of happiness from life, we would do well to honestly examine our life patterns and to adjust them accordingly to allow ourselves more room to relax, reflect, and become more responsible for all our activities.
—Matthew Culligan (quoted in Culligan & Sedlacek, 1976)

LEARNING OBJECTIVES

- I will understand how engaging in multiple life changes during a 12-month time span may impact my stress level.

- I will use the Recent Life Changes Questionnaire (RLCQ) every six months to determine how many points I have accumulated.

- I will recognize when my total RLCQ points are reaching a critical range and will then delay making further changes for at least six months.

- I will categorize the stressors I am encountering in my advising profession according to whether they are important, unimportant, changeable, or unchangeable and use coping prescriptions relevant for each category.

- I will check off the coping prescriptions for each of my stressors and practice those prescriptions daily.

Carl had just completed college and joined a brokerage firm with the goal of eventually becoming a full-service financial advisor. Following a long illness, his father, with whom Carl had been very close, died. Six months later, his long-time girlfriend broke up with him, citing his long working hours and the time he spent studying at home as reasons to end the relationship. Both of these events happened to him soon after he began taking classes in the evenings, working toward a master's degree in finance.

Soon after his girlfriend left, Carl was suffering from depression, anxiety, and fear related to losing his two most important support systems in six months. This depression manifested itself in sleeping difficulties and exhaustion, making getting to his office (which was located on the West Coast) by the time the market opened, a grueling task for him.

Carl was feeling overwhelmed and helpless. He contemplated quitting the job and even dropping out of school. Although he didn't know how he would earn a living, he thought that getting away from the job would relieve most of his stress. What happened to Carl? Read on to find out.

In their famous and widely published studies, Dr. Thomas Holmes and his colleague, Dr. Richard Rahe (1967a, 1967b), determined that specific events in people's lives tended to cause predictable levels of stress, and these events all had a common thread—the necessity to change their lives in some way (Holmes & Rahe, 1967a, 1967b). For example, changing jobs demands changes in one's life and is therefore stress provoking. In Carl's situation, losing a parent and a close relationship forced him to make major adjustments in his life. Even embarking on a much-anticipated evening educational program required adjustments, thus adding to his stress.

Dr. Mark Miller and Dr. Richard Rahe (1997) revised the social readjustment rating scale in 1997 and retitled it as the Recent Life Changes Questionnaire (RLCQ), which is found in Table 2.1.

As you can see, the RLCQ assigns a number of points to various events in a person's life according to the amount of change and adjustment that each event demands. These are called life change units (LCUs). The higher the LCU score (i.e., the more changes that are occurring in people's lives), the greater the risk of developing *distress* (strain), and therefore stress-related illnesses or emotional problems. Interestingly, many of the items on the questionnaire seem as if they would lead to *eustress* (Seyle, 1976), such as getting married, taking a vacation, or a job promotion. But, as you can imagine, each of these life events also requires a lot of adjusting and can therefore ultimately cause strain. You can score up to 199 points and still be relatively insulated from stress consequences.

So take an objective look at Table 2.1, and consider your life over the *past 12 months*. Put a check mark in the box next to any of the events that have occurred in your life and then total your LCU points, recording your score at the bottom.

In multiple studies (Hawkins, Davies, & Holmes, 1957; Holmes & Masuda, 1970; Holmes & Rahe, 1967b; Miller & Rahe, 1997), a clear relationship was established between the number of LCUs from events occurring over the previous 12 months and the onset of a disease, illness, or even being involved in an accident in the subsequent 12 months. Hence, scores from the past 12 months predict stress-related outcomes in the next 12 months.

Table 2.1   THE RECENT LIFE CHANGES QUESTIONNAIRE (RLCQ)

Health	
☐ An injury or illness that:	
☐ Kept you in bed a week or more or sent you to the hospital	74
☐ Was less serious than above	44
☐ Major dental work	26
☐ Major change in eating habits	27
☐ Major change in sleeping habits	26
☐ Major change in your usual type and/or amount of recreation	28
Work	
☐ Change to a new type of work	51
☐ Change in your work hours or conditions	35
☐ Change in your responsibilities at work	
☐ More responsibilities	29
☐ Fewer responsibilities	21
☐ Promotion	31
☐ Demotion	42
☐ Transfer	32

(Continued)

Table 2.1 (CONTINUED)	
Work	
☐ Trouble at work	
☐ With your boss	29
☐ With coworkers	35
☐ With persons under your supervision	35
☐ Other work troubles	28
☐ Major business adjustment	60
☐ Retirement	52
☐ Loss of job	
☐ Laid off from work	68
☐ Fired from work	79
☐ Correspondence course to help you in your work	18
Home and Family	
☐ Major change in living conditions	42
☐ Change in your responsibilities at work	
☐ Move in the same town or city	25
☐ Move to a different town, city, or state	47
☐ Change in family get-togethers	25
☐ Major change in health or behavior of a family member	55
☐ Marriage	50
☐ Pregnancy	67
☐ Miscarriage or abortion	65
☐ Gain of a new family member	
☐ Birth of a child	66
☐ Adoption of a child	65
☐ A relative moving in with you	59

Home and Family	
☐ Spouse beginning or ending work	46
☐ Child leaving home	
☐ To attend college	41
☐ Because of marriage	41
☐ Because of other reasons	45
☐ Change in arguments with spouse	50
☐ In-law problems	38
☐ Change in the marital status of your parents	
☐ Because of divorce	59
☐ Because of remarriage	50
☐ Separation from spouse	
☐ Because of work	53
☐ Because of marital problems	76
☐ Because of divorce	96
☐ Birth of a grandchild	43
☐ Death of spouse	119
☐ Death of other family member	
☐ Child	123
☐ Sibling	102
☐ Parent	100
Personal and Social	
☐ Change in personal habits	26
☐ Beginning or ending school or college	38
☐ Change of school or college	35
☐ Change in political beliefs	24
☐ Change in religious beliefs	29

(Continued)

Table 2.1 (CONTINUED)

Personal and Social	
☐ Change in social activities	27
☐ Vacation	24
☐ New, close, personal relationship	37
☐ Engagement to marry	45
☐ Girlfriend or boyfriend problems	39
☐ Sexual difficulties	44
☐ Falling out of a close personal relationship	47
☐ An accident	48
☐ Minor violation of the law	20
☐ Being held in jail	75
☐ Death of a close friend	70
☐ Major decision regarding your immediate future	51
☐ Major personal achievement	36
Financial	
☐ Major change in finances	
☐ Because of increased income	38
☐ Because of decreased income	60
☐ Because of investment and/or credit difficulties	56
☐ Loss or damage of personal property	43
☐ Moderate purchase	20
☐ Major purchase	37
☐ Foreclosure on a mortgage or loan	58

My Total Points for Events Taking Place in My Life in the Last 12 Months

Reprinted from *The Journal of Psychosomatic Research, Vol. 43,* Mark Miller and Richard Rahe, "Life changing scaling for the 1990s," pp. 279–292, 1997, with permission from Elsevier Publishing.

YOUR RECENT LIFE CHANGES SCORE AND ITS INTERPRETATIONS

Life events on the Holmes and Rahe scale are not necessarily good or bad.
They are simply times of extra strain.

—Keith Sedlacek (quoted in Culligan & Sedlacek, 1976)

Low LCU Score (0 to 199)

If your score falls in this range, your life changes in the past 12 months are relatively few in number and therefore relatively low in requirements for adjusting to change. Because of this low level of recent life changes, your risk for illness or an accident over the next year is also low. Only 10 percent of individuals in this range of life-change stress become ill in the subsequent 12 months.

In fact, if you score in this range, you might find yourself bored, irritable, and easily distracted, so consider adding some new challenges to your life. For example, take up a new hobby or learn something new.

Moderate LCU Score (200 to 299)

Most Americans report a moderate level of recent life changes, and these changes are indicative of a moderate level of strain. Each year, most Americans tend to experience some changes involving their work, living conditions, family and personal lives, and in their financial circumstances. Approximately 30 percent of those who experience a moderate LCU score will go on to develop a stress-related illness (physical or emotional) or accident in the next 12 months. Furthermore, the research suggests that this illness or accident will likely be one of moderate severity. If you score in this range, you probably find life interesting, challenging, and active most of the time. You may feel bored at times and stressed at other times.

Elevated LCU Score (300 to 449)

A yearly LCU score in this range is considered elevated and is associated with an elevated risk for an upcoming illness or accident. For persons in this range, approximately 50 percent will likely experience an illness or accident over the following year. More than one illness may also occur, and some of these illnesses may be severe. The strain on the body from elevated life changes can impair, among other things, normal immune function. For example, if you fall in this range, you may first develop allergies, then a cold, which could later progress into pneumonia.

High LCU Score (450 and Higher)

A high LCU score means not only that many life changes have taken place in the past 12 months, but also that some of these changes had very high-stress point values. Drs. Miller and Rahe (1997) refer to such high scores as a high-stress load, and they call it a "life crisis." Persons experiencing a life crisis have a 65 percent chance of developing one or more illnesses and/or accidents in the next 12 months. If your score falls in this category, put off any new changes you are contemplating to give your body and mind time to recoup. Let's say you have many LCU points and you are thinking about changing jobs, moving out of state, or even getting married. It may be best to delay those major changes until you have calmed down from the effects of the recent changes in your life.

You should also make sure that you engage in exercise, proper nutrition, relaxation exercises, and many of the other prescriptions you'll find in this book to help you manage your stress level, regardless of how high it is at that time in your life.

As you can imagine, this questionnaire is actually an *underestimate* of your stress because there are other events *not* listed on the RLCQ, some of which may have affected your life and caused major changes for you over the past 12 months. For example, think about the new wave of stress-provoking events taking a toll on Americans in the last few years: an economic recession, the bottom falling out of the housing and stock markets, record bank repossessions, the threat of global terrorism, the wars in Iraq and Afghanistan, and more and more natural disasters being attributed to the effects of global warming. None of these life-adjusting changes is represented in the RLCQ, so please understand that whenever you fill out the questionnaire, your score is most likely an *underestimate* of your actual stress level.

Good News!

Even if your LCU points are very high, you can delay many future life changes to ease the burden on you and your family.

Many life-changing events happen to us without warning and are not included on the questionnaire. For example, as I was working on my last book with a deadline from the publisher pending, my son walked in the door and announced that he was in an accident with our new car. This was an example of a life change thrust on me without warning and not part of the RLCQ. I had to get estimates, rent a replacement car to use while mine was being repaired, worry about my insurance rates, plus make sure my son wasn't traumatized by the whole affair.

The 2008 American Psychological Association's (APA) annual "Stress in America" survey, released in October 2008, found that 80 percent of Americans cited money and the economy as the top stressors they faced. Family health problems and job security fell closely behind and were in many ways related to the money and economy stressors. These life changes are not directly taken into account on the RLCQ either. Hopefully, when you are reading this book, the world will be stable and life for you will be thriving. But always be honest with yourself—whenever you score the RLCQ, if your life is filled with changes that are not included in it, heed the warning signs of an *underestimated* LCU score.

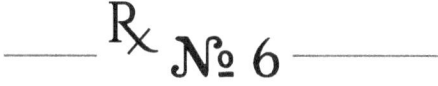

If you have had too much change on your plate in the last year, delay new changes that you can control for at least six months, such as tackling an evening course directed at attaining your MBA. Simply delay the course for several months and then engage in it.

By now, you've taken the questionnaire, scored it, and may be feeling overwhelmed or hopeless, right? You're bracing yourself for what you believe is the inevitable onset of an illness or accident. But hold the presses! Is there a stress-prone personality type that makes some advisors more vulnerable to these stressors? Can we learn how to increase the effectiveness of how we cope with the stressors that surround us? These questions all have answers that can help you to feel optimistic about your life, despite your score.

THE LIFE EVENT STRESSORS INHERENT IN ADVISING

Obviously, advisors not only have to deal with all of the life event changes delineated in the RLCQ—along with the stressors they are enduring in their nation and the world—but they also have a whole host of additional stressors to deal with every day.

Table 2.2 is a checklist of some potential job stressors inherent in advising. The stressors are categorized to help you logically examine the specific challenges you face in your job. You can view your potential stressors in the following categories: important/changeable, important/unchangeable, unimportant/changeable, and unimportant/unchangeable. I have filled in many potential stressors for you. Simply check off the ones you have to deal with and add ones that apply to you that are not included in the table.

Be careful to put the new ones in the correct box, according to importance and changeability.

Table 2.2 — CHECKLIST OF POTENTIAL JOB STRESSORS BY CATEGORY

Check all that apply to you, and add others that are not on the list.

Important/Changeable	*Unimportant/Changeable*
☐ Balancing time demands from your family	☐ *Time crunch in running errands before going home*
☐ Balancing time demands with clients	☐ *Volunteering to take on extra projects at the office*
☐ Fear of dealing with abusive and toxic clients	☐ *Work you prefer to complete in the office before going home*
☐ Feeling that no matter how hard you work on their behalf, it doesn't matter to some of your clients	
☐ Complaints from your manager	
☐ Staff inefficiency issues	
☐ Pressure to produce	
☐ Self-defeating thoughts about your future	
☐ Pessimism about your future	
☐ Worry about building your book of business	
☐ Emotional distance from your clients	
☐ Marital issues because of job stress	
☐ Fiduciary and compliance demands	
☐ The economy	

Important/Unchangeable	*Unimportant/Unchangeable*
☐ Volatile markets	☐ *Bad weather during your commute*
☐ An unsupportive manager	☐ *Traffic to and from the office*
☐ Terrorism	☐ *A colleague's book of business*
☐ Corporate scandals	
☐ Threat of inflation	
☐ Foreign crises	
☐ War	
☐ Family tragedy causing you to miss work	
☐ Chronic illness	

What is important here is your perception of the importance and changeability of each stressor. The more stressors you see as changeable, the more control you will feel. Frequently, we see stressors as out of our control when they really are not. Some creative thinking and brainstorming can go a long way toward recognizing that you have more control than you thought. In addition, we worry about important events over which we have no control. We must let go of those worries and move on.

Like the illustration of Brian in Chapter 1, examples of success stories will be revealed in each subsequent chapter.

Remember Carl? He had several unexpected events take place in his life in a short period, including the death of his father and his long-time girlfriend ending the relationship, blaming the long hours he committed to his job and night school. These events happened just when he began taking evening classes for his master's degree. Feeling overwhelmed and helpless, he contemplated quitting his job at the brokerage firm and even quitting school.

After consulting with me, I informed Carl about the life stressor research, and he then realized that making *additional* changes after the ones he'd already gone through in the past six months would only increase his stress, so he reluctantly decided to keep his job and stay in his master's program.

With my guidance, he began to examine his negative thinking, which was causing his depression and overwhelmed feelings. He used the Thinking-Pattern Worksheet (TPW) and the Thought-Stopping Technique (both coming up in Chapter 5) to change his whole outlook.

In three months, Carl was feeling much better, now recognizing that he could control some of his life stressors by avoiding major changes in his life. He focused on the positives, including developing more clients at work and excelling at school. Carl decided that although he missed both his father and girlfriend terribly, he could move on without them in his life. He surrounded himself with supportive friends from the office who helped him deal with the grind of the job, and he got closer to his older brother. Although he missed having a girlfriend in his life, he decided he would wait at least six months before exploring more relationship possibilities.

Within a year, Carl was thriving in both his job and in a new relationship.

Good News!

As you can see in Table 2.3, each chapter of this book is filled with practical, how-to methods of preventing or modifying your stress, regardless of its source. This table is your handy reference guide to examine coping prescriptions for virtually any job stressor that exists. Put a paper clip on this page so you can go back to it quickly whenever you need to.

Table 2.3 CHECKLIST OF COPING PRESCRIPTIONS BY STRESSOR CATEGORY

Check each prescription you review and use. Add new prescriptions you find useful.

Important/Changeable	*Unimportant/Changeable*
These types of job stressors are addressed best by assertively taking charge of each situation and making necessary changes, thus reducing stress. ☐ Develop time-management skills. (see Chapter 4) ☐ Maintain social support. (see Chapter 8)	*Because these potential stressors are perceived by you to be relatively unimportant, try to disregard them and let them go. If you find you can readjust these situations, go ahead and do it because you will feel better and it will perhaps build your confidence.* *All of the same skills described in the box to the left will work for these potential stressors, as well.*

Important/Changeable (cont.)	*Unimportant/Changeable*
☐ Use assertiveness skills. (see Chapter 4) ☐ Use active-listening skills with spouse, clients, and colleagues. (see Chapter 4) ☐ ☐ ☐	*same as previous page*
Important/Unchangeable	*Unimportant/Unchangeable*
These job stressors are the most difficult to deal with because they are important and you have no obvious way to control them. Left alone, these stressors can be overwhelming, lead to burnout, and lend to feelings of hopelessness and helplessness. But you can certainly do many things to help yourself, including changing the way you think about situations you can't change: ☐ Balance your life. (see Chapter 4) ☐ Focus on the positive aspects of your life. (see Chapter 3) ☐ Give yourself a "worry time." (If you must worry, each day allow yourself a maximum of 10 minutes to worry and always do it at the same time. Save all of your worrying for this time and do not allow yourself to worry for the rest of the day. Once your worry time is over for the day, focus on positive thinking). ☐ Maintain social support in and out of your office. (See Chapter 8)	*Since you view these potential stressors as unimportant, don't even bother with them.* *Everybody has these unpredictable hassles. Just go with the flow here and give yourself permission to ignore them.* *If you really must deal with these, you can use the same prescriptions described in the box to the left.*

(Continued)

Important/Unchangeable (cont.)	*Unimportant/Unchangeable*
☐ Maintain social support in and out of your office. (See Chapter 8) ☐ Practice relaxation techniques. (See Appendix C) ☐ Practice stress-hardiness techniques. (See Chapter 6) ☐ Recognize your negative thinking and distorted thoughts. It's fine to pay attention to the stressors you cannot change and come up with creative plans to deal with them, but it is completely overreacting to think doom-and-gloom catastrophic thoughts. The result will be that you will change your emotional reactions to these stressors. (See Chapter 3) ☐ Set goals and action plans for the future so you feel more in control. (See Chapter 6) ☐ Use the Thinking-Pattern Worksheet (TPW). (See Chapter 5) ☐ Use the Thought-Stopping Technique. (See Chapter 5) ☐ ☐ ☐	*Since you view these potential stressors as unimportant, don't even bother with them.* *Everybody has these unpredictable hassles. Just go with the flow here and give yourself permission to ignore them.* *If you really must deal with these, you can use the same prescriptions described in the boxes to the left.*

Good News!

Events in your life represent only about 10 percent of your stress. What you do about those events—particularly what you say to yourself about those events—represents the other 90 percent. Guess what? You can learn to control what you say to yourself about any event that befalls you. So smile and take a deep breath. Chapter 3 will teach you exactly how to do this.

℞ № 7

Let go of resentment you are holding toward anyone or anything. Don't harbor grudges. Forgive those who have hurt you and move on.

℞ № 8

For the next two weeks, keep a pad next to your bed. Each night, reflect on the day's activities and events. Write, on separate lines, at least five things you are grateful for that occurred during the last 24 hours.

ACTION PLAN FOR STRESS MASTERY

| Table 2.4 | My Action Plan for Stress Mastery |

Check each one when you've accomplished it. Feel free to add additional new behaviors in the spaces provided.

New Behavior	What I Did and the Date Accomplished
☐ I will mark my calendar to fill out the Recent Life Changes Questionnaire (RLCQ) every six months and total my points. ☐ ☐ ☐	What I did: Date accomplished:

(Continued)

| Table 2.4 | MY ACTION PLAN FOR STRESS MASTERY (CONT.) |

New Behavior	What I Did and the Date Accomplished
☐ If my points are too high for the last six months, I will delay making any major changes during the next six months. ☐ ☐ ☐	What I did: Date accomplished:
☐ I will categorize all of my job stressors into *important, unimportant, changeable,* and *unchangeable.* ☐ ☐ ☐	What I did: Date accomplished:
☐ I will look up the specific coping and preventive prescriptions to help me with each potential stressor I have. I will check off and practice at least one of those prescriptions daily. ☐ ☐	What I did: Date accomplished:

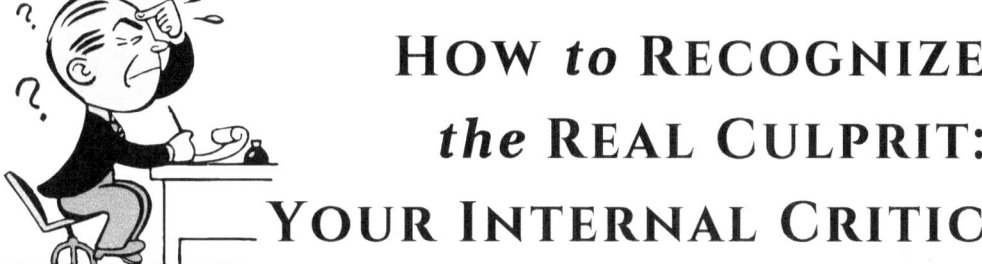

How to Recognize the Real Culprit: Your Internal Critic

All of us have collected thoughts and beliefs and ideas about ourselves that weigh us down and hold us back from reaching so many of the opportunities that life holds in store for us.
—Shad Helmstetter (1982)

LEARNING OBJECTIVES

- ✦ I will understand the origins of my beliefs and my internal critic.
- ✦ I will be able to explain the relationship between my thoughts, emotions, and behaviors.
- ✦ I will be able to examine my negative thoughts in the context of the 10 distorted self-talk patterns.
- ✦ Whenever I feel any negative emotion, I will be able to recognize the thoughts that led to that emotion, and then I will challenge those thoughts with nine key questions.
- ✦ Once I ask myself the nine key questions, I will use the A-B-C-D-E model to calm my emotions.
- ✦ I will make it a habit to focus my thinking on the things in life that I am grateful for, and of which I am proud.

UNDERSTANDING THE REAL CAUSES OF YOUR STRESS

Jay began his advising career as a single person, desiring to make enough money to feel comfortable financially. He navigated his way through this unpredictable career field, filled with market fluctuations and the struggle to build a steady book of business. Eventually he felt that his income was the best he could (or would) do. Jay may have been suffering from the "Impostor Fear," which you will learn about in this chapter.

After marrying and having three children, Jay realized that he needed to get serious about earning a substantial income. He was at a crossroads: Should he look for a more stable career, or take big risks in order to thrive in these choppy waters? At the end of this chapter, you will learn how Jay's career took a major turn.

Now allow me to also introduce you to Matt, who recently began an advising career after being encouraged by his father, a very successful advisor. Matt's father continually pointed to the wonderful lifestyle he provided for his family as an incentive for Matt to follow in his father's footsteps and eventually take over his book of business when he retired.

After marrying, Matt took his father's advice and embarked on an advising career, joining his father's firm. His dad was proud to introduce his son to his clients and tell them that one day he would retire and turn the reins over to Matt, at which point Matt would seamlessly step in and take over the successful counseling and planning role they had always experienced. In short, Matt's father told his clients that they should feel very comfortable putting their trust in Matt to manage and build their families' wealth.

This caused tremendous pressure for Matt. Although he loved the fact that the practice would be handed to him as soon as his father retired, he began to doubt whether he could do the same job his dad did for his clients. He began to think negative, irrational, self-defeating thoughts related to his abilities, such as:

- $ *My dad believes I'm more capable than I believe I am.*
- $ *I've been lucky so far in my career, but soon Dad's clients will realize that I don't have all the answers, I'll make mistakes advising them, and they'll view me as stupid. As soon as Dad retires, they'll change advisors. I can't do anything about this situation, and I feel inadequate and incompetent as an advisor.*
- $ *Once this happens, I won't be able to provide for my family. I feel terrible and don't know what to do. I'm feeling panicky right now.*

So what happened to Matt? Stay tuned …

As I noted in Chapter 2, it has been estimated that about 10 percent of the stress people feel at any time results from recent events in their lives, but a hefty 90 percent of the stress results from their internal dialogue related to those events (Helmstetter, 1982, 1987). Your self-talk determines whether an event in your life will lead to stress. This internal dialogue is based on your thinking habits and patterns, and these specific patterns of thoughts determine the degree of stress any event will provoke.

THE ORIGINS OF OUR BELIEF SYSTEMS

> *We are influenced not by "facts" but by our interpretation of facts.*
> —ALFRED ADLER, COLLEAGUE OF FREUD AND
> COFOUNDER OF THE PSYCHOANALYTIC MOVEMENT

Our beliefs and self-talk about any event that takes place in our lives are based on our habitual ways of looking at similar situations. It all starts with the words and phrases we use when talking to ourselves—our *inner dialogue.*

All of us have a little voice in our heads that we listen to hundreds of times a day. (If you happen to have more than one voice, call your local mental health specialist right away. ☺) Sadly, that voice inside our heads—more often than not—is filling our minds with negative, irrational, self-defeating statements, such as: *I'll never be able to do that*, or *I'm a failure,* or *I don't see any way to change my situation*.

Researcher and author Shad Helmstetter (1982, 1987) cites research showing that at least 75 percent of everything we think about is negative, self-defeating, pessimistic, and counterproductive. So many of our thoughts are self-defeating, not necessarily true, or based on inaccurate information, yet we continue to habitually fill our brains with scary, depressing, worrisome self-talk.

How did we develop these unfortunate thinking habits? The answer lies in fascinating research cited by Dr. Helmstetter (1982). By the time youngsters in the United States reach the age of 18, most have been negatively programmed with critical feedback, often by well-meaning parents, teachers, and other authority figures who believe they are helping those youngsters. Besides being told "no" or what we cannot do, we receive a great deal of negative programming, such as: "You aren't pretty enough to be chosen for homecoming queen, so don't embarrass yourself by trying"; "You won't make the football team"; "Music is not a major that will help you in life, so don't waste your time"; "That's too risky, so don't attempt it"; "Don't worry, I don't expect you to do well anyway"; or "Why can't you be more like your sister?"

From my own experience, a misinformed high school guidance counselor once told my parents, "Jack is not college material, so you can save the money you would have spent on tuition and prepare him for a trade instead." Later, you'll learn how I turned those absurd comments from a "professional" into personal motivation.

Helmstetter (1982) claims that during the first 18 years of life, most of us have heard negatives from these people at least 148,000 times, in contrast to only a few thousand positive comments about what we *can* do or accomplish in life. It's no wonder then that with this ratio of 148,000 negatives to 3,000 or 4,000 positives, most of us are programmed to think negatively, fear taking risks, have low self-confidence and self-esteem, and tend to be constantly critical of ourselves. In short, this is the beginning of the development of what I call our *internal critic*.

You might think that once we grow older, we are no longer under the influence of the early life programming from our parents, teachers, and others who "care" about us. But sadly, most of us pick right up where that negative programming left off. In other words, we continue to beat ourselves up with the same negative, self-critical, distorted thoughts that were originally "planted" into our subconscious minds by others. As one of my cherished mentors, Dr. Lee Pulos (2004), put it:

> The subconscious mind is like a garden full of beautiful flowers. Sadly, we have had weeds planted in that garden by well-meaning, but misinformed parents, teachers, siblings and other people with whom we interact ... and then we continue to fertilize and water those weeds with our own habitual negative thoughts and beliefs. (From a paper presented at a meeting of the American Society of Clinical Hypnosis, Denver, Colorado)

As we continue to beat ourselves up with an internal dialogue of self-doubt, worry, fear, and lack of confidence, our belief systems, attitudes, and behaviors develop our *internal critic*. See Figure 3.1 for an illustration.

This cycle of negativity, beginning with the words from our parents, siblings, teachers, and others, establishes the foundation of our belief systems, attitudes, emotions, and behaviors, which is habitually reinforced in our minds, by us. So it's not the events, but our habitual, negative *internal interpretation* of those events that ultimately leads to our stress.

Here's what we know about internal thoughts, or *self-talk*. Helmstetter (1987) reports that neuroscientists have proof that all "thoughts are electrical impulses that trigger electrical and chemical switches in the brain" (p. 14). Whenever a thought takes place, the brain releases chemicals to set off specific additional chemical, electrical, and physical responses in the body. If a thought is negative or frightening, these physical responses switch on the sympathetic nervous system (SNS), causing what Seyle (1976) called the stress-response syndrome to take place. If the thought is positive, encouraging, and optimistic, the parasympathetic nervous system is triggered, leading us to feel calm, confident, and happy.

> **Figure 3.1** — **THE ORIGINS AND CONSEQUENCES OF OUR INTERNAL CRITIC**
>
> - From our parents and other significant adults, we become programmed with negative, self-defeating ideas about ourselves, and as a result our INTERNAL CRITIC is formed.
>
> - We pick up where they left off and continue to fuel our internal critic with our own negative SELF-TALK.
>
> - Our negative SELF-TALK creates negative BELIEFS.
>
> - Our negative beliefs create negative ATTITUDES.
>
> - Our negative attitudes create negative FEELINGS, MOODS, and EMOTIONS.
>
> - Our negative feelings, moods, and emotions create negative BEHAVIORS and even negatively affect our immune system.
>
> - Our negative behaviors are self-fulfilling prophecies, and they fuel the negative, self-defeating thoughts that make up our internal critic, so this is a CONTINUOUS CIRCLE,
>
> *Unless we intervene in the process.*

It's important to understand that our subconscious mind always takes orders from us and simply records what it receives. It doesn't matter if the thought was based on reality, a lie, or a distortion of reality. As an example, if you close your eyes and imagine yourself lying on a beach in Hawaii, with the turquoise ocean in front of you, a gentle breeze coming off the water, and feeling the rays of the sun warming your body, you can eventually feel a calming, comfortable feeling come over you as these images trigger the parasympathetic nervous system. This type of visualizing is actually the basis for the power of hypnosis. Again, your subconscious mind doesn't know the difference between *actual* and *imagined* images or thoughts. It goes with whatever you put into it, good or bad, without judging it. As Helmstetter (1987) puts it: "Your subconscious mind will not care where that programming comes from or how it gets it. It will just continue to accept the input that is fed to it—right or wrong, for better or worse" (p. 18).

Repeating the same negative, self-critical thoughts to ourselves whenever we are in a similar situation develops a pattern of repeated, stress-causing reactions in our brains.

> The brain makes no moral judgments; it simply accepts what you tell it ... It makes no difference whether the things you have told yourself or believed about yourself in the past were true or not. The brain doesn't care! (Helmstetter, 1982, p. 59)

Self-talk habits develop connections in your subconscious mind between situations, your interpretation of those situations, and immediate chemical and electrical connections to the appropriate nervous system. So it's critical to understand and take charge of your self-talk habits.

Taking command of your self-talk, regardless of past programming from others and reinforcement from your thinking habits, can develop *new programming* in your subconscious mind. It is up to you. You really can change those thinking habits!

Good News!
Repeating positive, healthy thoughts to yourself can permanently change the mental connections established by your old thinking habits.

THE YOUNG FINANCIAL ADVISOR'S GREATEST CHALLENGE: OVERCOMING THE IMPOSTOR FEAR

A common self-talk issue that haunts many financial advisors when they are new to the career is telling themselves that the rigors and requirements of the profession, beginning with the licensing requirements, may be more than they can handle. If they come from a background of things coming easily to them in college and now they find this grind difficult, their self-talk may begin to undermine their confidence. They may suffer extreme anxiety and/or depression as a result of thinking such self-defeating thoughts as: *My manager made a mistake hiring me* or *I don't really have what it takes* or *I'll be humiliated when he fires me.*

When in the throes of feeling like an "impostor" (Clance, 1985) who soon will be exposed, the young advisor views any success as "lucky" and temporary. The good news is that most fears are easily overcome by developing healthy thinking habits and taking setbacks on the job as challenges that can be overcome, rather than feeling overwhelmed by them.

When my guidance counselor told my parents that I wasn't college material, I had two choices: I could have either accepted the opinion of this "expert" and resigned myself to the "fact" that I didn't have what it takes to succeed in college, or I could have stood at that crossroad in my life and told myself that he was dead wrong about me and I could prove it. Fortunately for me, I chose the second path.

Many years later, after earning a bachelor's and master's degree, a PhD, a post doctorate, and several individual honors, I returned to my high school to show my diplomas to that counselor. I told him that he needed to be careful what he said to students and their families. His words certainly could have destroyed my future, and they may very well have destroyed the futures of others who simply gave up.

Table 3.1 gives examples of self-talk that provoke negative emotions and stress. Many of these thoughts could have originated with comments from your parents, for example, and then were reinforced by your restating those thoughts hundreds of times to yourself over the years. Are you a victim of any of these self-talk examples?

Table 3.1 EXAMPLES OF STRESS-PROVOKING, DISTORTED SELF-TALK

I'm not nearly as good as the other advisors in my office.

My future as an advisor looks bleak.

Everything I do turns out badly.

I feel so much resentment, envy, fear, and sadness.

I'm feeling hopeless.

I have no control over my destiny.

No one can help me feel better.

No one really cares about me the way I need them to.

I've always failed, and this is another example.

I'm stupid, and I'll never figure out what to do about my situation.

OUR SELF-TALK AND OUR EMOTIONS

There's nothing either good or bad but thinking makes it so.

—WILLIAM SHAKESPEARE, HAMLET

As you now understand, stress is *not* about what happens to you. Stress results from what you *say to yourself* about what happens to you. You can choose to think in a healthy fashion, regardless of what kinds of thoughts you have allowed to enter your subconscious mind, unchallenged, in the past. William James, famous American philosopher and psychologist, said it best: "The greatest weapon against stress is our ability to choose one thought over another." (2009)

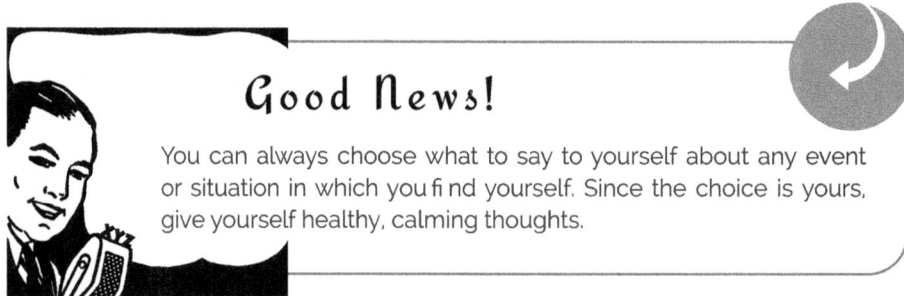

Good News!

You can always choose what to say to yourself about any event or situation in which you find yourself. Since the choice is yours, give yourself healthy, calming thoughts.

Let's revisit the unhealthy, stress-provoking examples in Table 3.1 and replace them with the rational, optimistic, self-talk examples in Table 3.2.

Table 3.2 — EXAMPLES OF HEALTHY, RATIONAL SELF-TALK

Practice saying these affirmations out loud.

"I have special skills that make me a real asset as an advisor."

"My future as an advisor looks great. I don't have to be perfect to be an excellent advisor."

"I make mistakes like everyone else, but I learn from them."

"I experience negative emotions, but I find ways to release them quickly and move on."

"No matter what happens in my life, I will remain optimistic that new opportunities for success and happiness are just around the corner."

> "I control the thoughts in my mind, and I choose to stop negative thoughts quickly and replace them with positive ones."
>
> "I am ultimately responsible for the way I feel because I am in control of my thinking. I choose to forgive others and to forgive myself for mistakes I've made."
>
> "Right now, I'm not where I'd ultimately like to be in my financial advising career, but I will hold positive images and goals in my mind, as well as pictures of what I truly want. I'm confident that sooner or later, I'll skyrocket my career through world-class client service, including listening to my clients and collaborating with them to give them secure feelings about their wealth management issues."
>
> "When I've failed in the past, it has been because of my negative programming. I now know how to move beyond those thoughts and to be successful. It just takes practice and consistency."
>
> "I'm smart enough to realize where my thinking has caused my problems in the past and what I need to do to change those habits."

℞ № 9

Recognize that you are not a prisoner of past programming. Just because you heard negative comments from your parents and others does not make those statements accurate. You can choose to disregard them, and you can decide not to repeat them to yourself. Instead, repeat healthy, optimistic thoughts to yourself daily.

♦ ♦ ♦

It's reasonable to assume that there is a direct cause-and-effect relationship between an event or situation people find themselves in, and their emotional reactions to that event. For example, let's say that it is shortly after the 2008 economic crisis and you are told by your assistant that your most difficult/toxic client is demanding to have a meeting with you. Let's say that this is the final straw for you. You have decided to resign from the advising profession. Using information from Figure 3.2, one might assume that the prospect of your having that meeting with the client was the activating event (A) that caused you to feel the stressful emotions of hopelessness and helplessness (C1), and those feelings could lead to the stressful behavioral reaction of considering quitting your profession (C2).

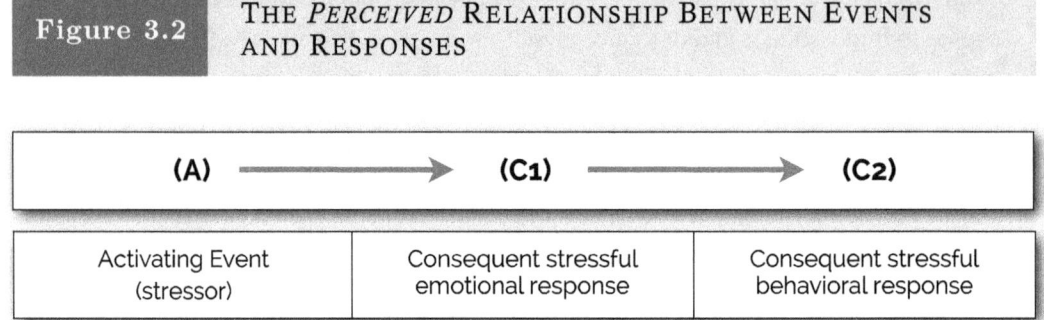

Figure 3.2 — THE *PERCEIVED* RELATIONSHIP BETWEEN EVENTS AND RESPONSES

(A) → (C1) → (C2)

| Activating Event (stressor) | Consequent stressful emotional response | Consequent stressful behavioral response |

Because of a tremendous volume of research in the area of Cognitive/Behavioral Therapy, much of which is found in Dr. David Burns' book, *The Feeling Good Handbook* (1989), it has now been well established that your *thoughts, beliefs, and attitudes—not* the events and situations in which you find yourself—create and cause your emotional reactions and your resultant behavioral responses. This relationship can be understood best using the **A-B-C** model in Figure 3.3.

Figure 3.3 — THE *ACTUAL* RELATIONSHIP BETWEEN EVENTS, BELIEFS ABOUT EVENTS, AND EMOTIONAL AND BEHAVIORAL RESPONSES TO EVENTS (THE STRESS RESPONSE)

(A) ⟶ (B)

| Activating Event | Beliefs about the event |

(C1) ⟶ (C2)

| Consequent stressful emotional response | Consequent stressful behavioral response |

As you can see, it's *not* the activating event or stressor (A), per se, that produces the consequent emotions and behaviors (C1, C2), but it is *your belief about* or *interpretation of that event* (B) that causes the consequent emotional (C1) and behavioral (C2) reactions.

You can easily remember this process using the equation in Figure 3.4.

Figure 3.4 SIMPLIFIED EQUATION OF THE STRESS RESPONSE RELATIONSHIP

$$(A) + (B) = (C1) + (C2)$$

Any event *plus* your beliefs about the event *leads to* your emotional and behavioral reactions to that event.

So when you learned about this client demanding a meeting (A), you immediately began to think about yourself and the situation at hand in a negative, pessimistic way (B). You began to tell yourself that you would not be able to pacify this client and he would make threatening gestures about removing his account from you. It would only be the beginning, you predicted. Other clients would be disenchanted with you and jump ship. It was these *thoughts* that caused you to feel stressed (C1). After consulting with some equally pessimistic colleagues who were also considering resigning, these thoughts were reinforced and, ultimately, your emotions reached a level where you thought your only relief from the situation would come from writing a resignation letter to your manager (C2).

Clearly, your negative *thoughts* about your situation and your inner dialogue led to your emotional and behavioral reactions. Those reactions were *not* simply the result of the anticipated meeting with the client (the event). You had choices as to what to say to yourself about the situation. As examples, here are some alternative thoughts you could have given to yourself:

I've been in difficult dilemmas before and found creative ways to solve them. I cannot please everyone, so I'll focus on the clients who trust me and with whom I can easily communicate. I've been told by those clients in the past that I'm a wonderful advisor and they're very happy to entrust their families' wealth to me. I don't have to please every single client to consider myself a success.

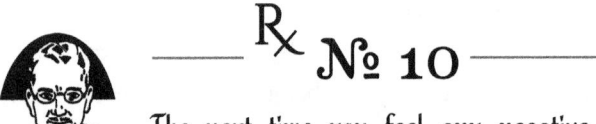

Rx № 10

The next time you feel any negative emotion (overwhelm, depression, irritation, impatience, or hopelessness), list the specific thoughts that went through your mind just before you felt that emotion. This is the first step in recovering from your stress.

EXPOSE AND DISPOSE OF YOUR INTERNAL CRITIC

If you are pained by an external thing, it is not this external thing that disturbs you, but your own judgment about it. And it is in your own power to wipe out this judgment now.

—MARCUS AURELIUS, PHILOSOPHER

To challenge our internal critic and render it impotent, we need to understand our distorted-thinking patterns and the alternative thoughts we have available to us. As I pointed out earlier, the "weeds" that were planted in our subconscious minds by our parents and other authority figures were then "watered and fertilized" by us as we perpetuated those unfortunate thinking habits.

COMMON NEGATIVE SELF-TALK PATTERNS

If you want to break out of a bad mood, you must first understand that every type of negative feeling results from a specific kind of negative thought.

—DR. DAVID BURNS (1989)

We now know that our internal critic consists of persistent patterns of negative, self-defeating thoughts that we quickly employ when we encounter difficult situations or events. Learning about these unfortunate, distorted-thinking patterns is the first step in making life-altering changes in our thinking. The definitions of these patterns are based on the pioneering work by Dr. Matt McKay (1981) and Dr. David Burns (1989). Ten common negative-thinking patterns are found in Table 3.3. Copy the table and keep it handy for quick reference.

| Table 3.3 | TEN NEGATIVE SELF-TALK PATTERNS |

Self-Talk Pattern	Example of Internal Dialogue (Check if you believe you are thinking this way)
☐ All or nothing	*If I can't please every one of my clients, I'm a failure.*
☐ Magnification	*It would be really awful if any of my clients didn't have faith in me.*
☐ Mind reading	*If my colleague is irritated, it must be because of something I've done or said.*
☐ Catastrophizing or fortune-telling	*What if I can't build my book of business during the present economic challenges? I will fail and have to quit this job.*
☐ Having to be right	*I don't care what the rules say. If I have an abusive client, I have the right to be just as abusive right back at him.*
☐ I should, I must, I have to	*I should be to able handle the multiple roles of advisor, attorney, and marriage counselor for clients. That's my job.*
☐ Mental filter	*I don't care how many clients praise me. Even if only one criticizes me, I can't get that out of my mind. I'm a failure.*
☐ Overgeneralization	*I always have trouble asserting myself with my clients, and this will continue.*
☐ Blaming	*My poor evaluation was only because my manager doesn't like me.*
☐ Emotional reasoning	*How could I make the same mistake twice? I really must be stupid.*

ALL-OR-NOTHING THINKING

With this distorted thinking, you look at your world as strictly black or white, good or bad. Such thinking often involves attempting to be perfect, which is obviously impossible. You believe if you can't do something perfectly, then you have failed.

Example: An advisor has an annual client appreciation event and meets and greets all of her clients. All but two of them heap praise on her for the wonderful work she is doing with their wealth management. The advisor then asks herself, *How can I call myself a good financial advisor when two of my clients are unhappy with me? Maybe I'm not cut out for this profession.*

MAGNIFICATION

In this distortion, you take things out of perspective and dramatically intensify what is actually happening. You use dramatic words like *awful*, *disgusting*, and *terrible* to describe situations and outcomes that are rarely that critical. This magnification of what is actually happening leads to scenarios such as the following:

An advisor goes to a staff meeting and learns about new governmental compliance and fiduciary requirements coming down the pike. He then says to himself, *This is awful. The amount of paperwork required for me to service my clients is getting unbearable!*

The reality is that the new compliance and fiduciary issues are a pain, but it's unlikely that these requirements are really *awful* or *unbearable*—terms that should be reserved for really bad situations, like natural disasters or losing one's job. We call this tendency to magnify *awfulizing*.

MIND READING

This is a very common pattern. You conclude that you somehow have an ESP-like understanding of what people are feeling and thinking about you and surmise that people you know are thinking or feeling something negative about you. Even though you have no real evidence to support this conclusion, you just "feel" it, so you believe it to be true.

A classic example: An advisor is told that her manager would like to speak to her during the lunch break. The advisor immediately asks herself: *What did I do wrong? I must be in some kind of trouble here.*

CATASTROPHIZING OR FORTUNE-TELLING

The tip-off to this pattern is the use of "what ifs." You take a situation or event and blow it out of proportion by *assuming* that a disastrous outcome is on its way. You come to expect a catastrophic conclusion, as if you have a crystal ball to look into the future and (of course) expect that outcome to be something negative.

In the previous example, the advisor not only assumes that her manager is upset with her, but she starts to worry about being fired. *Oh my gosh*, she thinks, *what if my manager is calling me in to fire me? How will I tell my husband? And what about our family? How can we support them when I lose my job? Will we need to go on welfare? And how will this look to my parents and our friends?*

You can imagine how such catastrophic thoughts can easily lead to the emotions of despair, hopelessness, and fear. The result, in terms of behavior, could be avoidance of the fear-producing situation, such as avoiding speaking with your manager by finding reasons to leave the office during lunch breaks and at the end of the day. The advisor could even begin to develop vague physical symptoms, leading to increased absences—all psychologically to avoid the manager.

HAVING TO BE RIGHT

Having to be right *all of the time* develops out of insecurity. This is based on a fear of what people will think about you if you are wrong. Therefore, you don't listen to another person's point of view or logic that may prove your position on an issue to be wrong. After all, you don't know how to deal with being wrong.

An example is an advisor who feels threatened by questions from one of his assertive clients about whether he has been doing his homework, researching new products that would fit the client's portfolio. Because the advisor has been negligent in this regard and since he has the need to be right, he ignores the client and focuses on clients who never question or challenge him.

I SHOULD, I MUST, AND I HAVE TO

People who frequently use words like these in their thinking are making an unconscious assumption that there is a universal list of ironclad rules (besides the laws of the land and your particular religious commandments) to which we must all adhere. If you break the rule (*I shouldn't have done that*), it leads to feelings of guilt. If someone else breaks the rule (*She should have done this*), it results in your feeling frustrated or angry.

Although we often regret actions that brought unfortunate outcomes, and we may use the word *should* on ourselves, the *continual* use of such words leaves no room for innocent mistakes. There is no room here to give yourself a break.

An advisor can actually talk himself or herself out of a good career with misplaced blame, as in this example: After the economic disaster of 2008, an advisor takes personal responsibility for the losses her clients suffered. She beats herself up unmercifully with self-talk such as, *I should have anticipated this disaster and put my clients in safer products. I'm incompetent and shouldn't be advising.*

MENTAL FILTER

This form of distorted thinking involves having tunnel vision when it comes to positives in your life. You can have ten positive things happen, but you dwell only on the single negative experience you had.

Here's an example of such thinking, which almost everyone has experienced to a degree: An advisor gets a very good performance review from his manager, but there is a single comment from the manager suggesting that the advisor bring in more clients. Instead of focusing on all of the positive feedback, the advisor comes away from the meeting highly upset. He can't stop thinking thoughts such as, *I feel like a failure, and my manager is upset with me.* (This is also an example of "mind reading" and "all-or-nothing" thinking.)

OVERGENERALIZATION

You have an unfortunate incident, and you believe it is the beginning of a never-ending pattern of similar episodes. The tip-off to this kind of thinking is the frequent use of words such as *never, always, all, every, and none*. These absolutes are exaggerations of reality, and they are extremely self-defeating.

One can get carried away with this type of thinking. For example: An advisor is informed that one of her more difficult clients is requesting a meeting as soon as possible. Instead of assuming this is a normal business meeting where the client wants to discuss her financial planning situation, the advisor says to herself: *This client always gives me aggravation. I can never please him.* (This is also fortune-telling.)

BLAMING

This in an interesting example of distorted thinking because there is some fascinating research suggesting you may actually want to find someone or something to blame when you fail to accomplish something important to you. As you will discover in Chapter 8, there are often decided advantages to finding an excuse to explain failure rather than blaming yourself, as if you are incompetent. It's detrimental, however, when you *constantly* berate yourself for every unhappy or unfortunate situation that befalls you or you rarely take responsibility and quickly blame others for your misfortunes.

Ultimately, it's about holding ourselves accountable. For example: An advisor is criticized by a client for failing to follow the client's wishes. Instead of accepting the criticism, admitting his mistake, planning how to accomplish the client's goals at this point, and understanding that this feedback will help him to become a better advisor, he internally blames the client and tells himself this client will never be pleased, saying *It's not my fault.*

EMOTIONAL REASONING

This example of distorted thinking involves drawing the wrong conclusion based on your emotions at the time. Because you feel an emotion or have a thought, you conclude that it must be true. For example, if you make a mistake and *feel* stupid, you conclude, *I must be stupid.* If you feel anger, you conclude that the person in question must have done something bad to you, rather than realizing that your angry emotions may be based on faulty thinking or not having all of the information.

Here's an example: An advisor compares his book of business to those of his colleagues in the office. Even though he is making a good living, he feels like a failure because his business lags behind all of his colleagues. Since he tells himself that he is failing compared to his colleagues, he begins to feel like a failure. This kind of self-defeating belief could deteriorate his confidence, making it even harder for him to go after business.

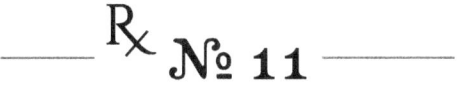

Recognize the specific negative self-talk patterns you have developed. Make a list of typical negative thoughts you have in an average day and check the list of 10 common distorted-thinking patterns to determine which ones you engage in regularly.

The most important step in the process of eliminating the emotional, physical, and behavioral consequences of adverse events in our lives is recognizing the distortions in our thinking and beliefs about those events. The next step is challenging—or *disputing*—those thoughts. You don't have to believe your negative and scary thoughts; they lie and can mislead, tease, and frighten you. Just because they cross your mind doesn't make them true.

You can ask yourself several key questions regarding each of your thoughts that belongs to a negative-thinking pattern. Copy Table 3.4 so you will have these key questions for quick reference to challenge your negative thoughts.

Table 3.4 QUICK REFERENCE GUIDE OF QUESTIONS TO CHALLENGE YOUR NEGATIVE THINKING

- *What negative situation am I assuming is (or will be) happening to me?*
- *What is the evidence to support my conclusions?*
- *Could I be exaggerating the situation in my mind?*
- *Am I turning a minor setback into a major catastrophe in my mind?*
- *Is there any alternative explanation that could explain what happened or what will happen next? Could I be confusing facts with recurring thoughts in my mind?*
- *Are my conclusions based on emotions rather than on facts?*
- *Can I really predict the future?*
- *Am I using extreme words and phrases in my thoughts?*
- *Am I assuming the worst will happen without evidence of that?*

What negative situation am I assuming is (or will be) happening to me?

Try to identify the specific situation, event, or concern that triggered your negative thoughts in the first place. It's usually about bad things that have happened in the past or frightening things you believe will take place in the future.

What is the evidence to support my conclusions?

If you are just starting out as a financial professional and you conclude after one month that you will never be successful, where is the evidence to support that belief? Can you be 100 percent certain of this conclusion? Perhaps you haven't been successful (whatever that constitutes in your mind) up until now, but by learning from and brainstorming with your colleagues, you may very well learn the tricks of the trade to be quite successful down the road.

Could I be exaggerating the situation in my mind?

Perfectionistic thinkers tend to talk to themselves in terms of certainties. *The manager looks upset. She must be angry with me.* You react as if there is 100 percent certainty of your conclusion from the manager's expressions or behavior. If you ask yourself what the probability is that she is mad at you based on all of the information you have, you'll be surprised at how quickly you can dismiss what you earlier concluded was a certainty. Most of us tend to exaggerate the inevitability of bad outcomes and minimize the chances of good outcomes resulting from the situation we're in.

Am I turning a minor setback into a major catastrophe in my mind?

Everyone has unfortunate things that happen to them in their lives. Moreover, life is unpredictable, and you never know when these things will happen. For example, a financial professional may have to deal with a disgruntled client who says offensive things to the professional during a face-to-face meeting. This does not mean any more than that client has an issue with events that affected her money. Don't take that specific situation and the comments the client made to you, which could be more a reflection of the issues that person has in general, and blow it out of proportion, put yourself down, and/or decide that your skills are lacking.

Is there any alternative explanation that could clarify what happened or what will happen next? Could I be confusing facts with recurring thoughts in my mind?

Often, we *assume* that something is true because we keep thinking about it in the same way. For example, if you frequently believe that your manager doesn't like you, you may believe it because you habitually think that way, but you probably don't have facts to prove whether your perception is accurate. Remember, your thoughts are not always based on facts but more on emotions, and we tend to habitually repeat the same thoughts to ourselves unless we recognize that they are distorted or not based on facts. Your thoughts are frequently the result of fears or fantasies and not based on the facts of the situation.

Are my conclusions actually based on my emotions rather than on facts?

The danger here is observing your feelings and emotions and concluding that they validate your thoughts. *Because I'm nervous and frightened every time the manager observes me with a client, there must be something I'm doing wrong and I have reason to be afraid. So because I'm afraid of what she'll see, I'm sure she's looking for grounds to fire me.* This kind of thinking can lead to performance anxiety every time the manager enters your office to observe; thus, you have a self-fulfilling prophecy, which reinforces this vicious cycle of anxiety-producing thinking and the resultant frightening feelings.

Can I really predict the future?

Just because something unfortunate happened when you were in this situation before doesn't mean it is guaranteed to happen again. Think about all of the other possible outcomes that could take place next time.

Am I using extreme words and phrases in my thoughts?

As I mentioned earlier, people often think in extremes and use terms such as *always, forever, never, should,* and *must* when they describe the way they see things. It's important to recognize when you are thinking this way and replace those words in your mind to words like *often* and *sometimes*.

Am I assuming the worst will happen without evidence to support that assumption?

Few situations are black or white, and you are neither perfect nor a failure. Look at your situation without imagining extremes or thinking about the worst thing that could happen, as if it is guaranteed to happen just because it crossed your mind.

Once you answer these key questions for yourself, you are on your way to exploring the specific distorted-thinking patterns that you may be using. Then, when you recognize the habitual, distorted-thinking pattern habits you use, you can develop rational rebuttals or disputes of your original thinking.

 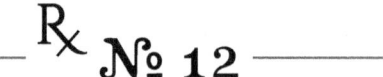

Whenever you recognize that you are upset and thinking negatively, use the quick reference guide of questions to challenge that negative thinking.

Figure 3.5 — THE A-B-C-D-E MODEL

(A) → (B) → (C) → (D) → (E)

| Activating event (stressor) | Beliefs (thoughts) about the event | Consequent emotions and behaviors | Disputing thoughts | Energized, revitalized emotions |

The A-B-C model now becomes the A-B-C-D-E model (Figure 3.5). Once we recognize the distortions in our beliefs and thoughts, we can *dispute* or challenge those beliefs and thoughts (D), which then greatly diminishes the consequences (C) that arose before you realized your thinking was distorted. The result is positive, energized, and revitalized emotions (E). In Chapter 5, you will find a convenient form called the Thinking-Pattern Worksheet (TPW), which is a handy way of recognizing distorted thought patterns and disputing them.

Remember Jay, the advisor who began his career feeling content making ends meet until he found himself with four additional mouths to feed? He was at a critical juncture in his life where he needed to either move on to a more steady career with a predictable income, or believe and trust in himself that he could be a success as an advisor.

Jay pulled himself out of feeling like an impostor and took charge of his "Internal Critic." He realized that inviting mentors into his life was wise and didn't suggest weakness, so he attached himself to a wonderful general manager in the firm who showed Jay how to believe in himself and how to feel comfortable out of his "comfort zone." Jay attributes two of his personality traits with re-inventing himself: patience and persistence.

In addition, Jay:

- hired a referral coach
- hired an assistant and allowed himself to delegate responsibility, giving him more time for rainmaking
- hired a business manager
- instituted a monthly marketing plan with specific goals
- developed self-discipline to balance his time between his job and family
- assertively persisted with potential clients—even if they were happy with their current advisor—because their advisor could retire, they could change jobs and need a 401K established, or they could become disenchanted with their advisor

- got organized by using a contact management program
- assertively asked his friends and family for names of contacts who might benefit from sitting down with Jay to discuss their financial plans and goals
- had annual reviews in a proactive way, with each client

Jay is now a qualifying and lifetime member of Million Dollar Round Table (MDRT) with 15 consecutive qualifications and two Court of Table qualifications.

What about Matt, who saw himself as an impostor in the advising profession? Matt sought my counsel primarily because he wanted to abandon his advising career and was afraid to tell his father about this decision. As discussed in this chapter, Matt was suffering from a classic case of "Impostor Fear." He was afraid that it was only a matter of time before his father's clients would realize that Matt did not have what it took to entrust their accounts with him. He attributed the success he had achieved up to that point to "luck" and to his belief that his clients were likely hoping that his dad would train him, so they would hang on for a while longer. This led to sleeplessness, fatigue, bouts of anxiety, and a dread of coming to work on Mondays.

I began my work with Matt by asking him to trust me and my expertise, strongly suggesting that he not quit his job until he and I had at least two months to work together. Matt reluctantly agreed.

Our work began with Matt learning how his negative self-talk had led to his panicky feelings and the belief that he would ultimately be exposed for the impostor he felt he was. Matt understood that his habitual negative thinking patterns included Catastrophizing, All-or-Nothing thoughts, Mind Reading, Overgeneralization, Emotional Reasoning, and Self-Blame (that's quite a list, isn't it?).

Matt learned the A-B-C-D-E model to expose and dispose of his "Internal Critic." Soon he could catch himself when his thinking began to head down one of these self-defeating roads and quickly dispute the irrationality of the thought. For example, whenever he felt inadequate as an advisor, he reminded himself of the following identity statement: *I am diligent about doing careful research regarding any product I recommend for my clients. Of course, I cannot predict market or economic fluctuations, which could affect the value of these products; however, I have explained why each recommendation I make is for the long haul. I'm proud of my commitment to my clients to listen, respect, collaborate, and serve them and their families.*

After the two-month commitment to remaining in his position, Matt was sleeping better, looking forward to coming to the office on Mondays, and enthusiastic about his future in his chosen career. His father gave him constant, positive feedback from clients about his work, and Matt couldn't be happier with his performance.

ACTION PLAN FOR STRESS MASTERY

Table 3.5 — My Action Plan for Stress Mastery

Check each one when you've accomplished it. Feel free to add additional new behaviors in the spaces provided.

New Behavior	What I Did and the Date Accomplished
☐ Every day I will remember that I have choices regarding how I think about myself and my life. I can choose to disregard the negative comments about me that my parents and others said. ☐ ☐ ☐	What I did: Date accomplished:
☐ I choose not to repeat those negative comments to myself. ☐ ☐ ☐	What I did: Date accomplished:
☐ I will make a list of the things in my life that I am grateful for, pin that list above my computer or on my refrigerator, and look at it and add to it each day. ☐ ☐ ☐	What I did: Date accomplished:

(Continued)

| Table 3.5 | MY ACTION PLAN FOR STRESS MASTERY (CONT.) |

New Behavior	What I Did and the Date Accomplished
☐ Anytime I feel a negative emotion (overwhelm, depression, irritation, impatience, or hopelessness), I will list the specific thoughts that preceded that emotion and use the A-B-C-D-E model to calm my emotions down. ☐ ☐ ☐	What I did: Date accomplished:
☐ I will make a list of common negative thoughts that I have in a typical day and check the list of 10 common distorted thinking patterns to determine which ones I engage in regularly. ☐ ☐ ☐	What I did: Date accomplished:
☐ I will challenge my distorted thoughts by using the nine key questions found in this chapter. ☐ ☐ ☐	What I did: Date accomplished:

4

HOW *to* THRIVE DESPITE BEING GENETICALLY WIRED *with* STRESS-PRONE PERSONALITY TRAITS

*We know now beyond any doubt what we suspected before—
that Type-A behavior can be treated effectively.*

—MEYER FRIEDMAN AND DIANE ULMER (1984)

LEARNING OBJECTIVES

- I will determine whether I exhibit any of the Type-A behaviors, and if so, I will choose those behaviors I wish to modify and use the steps discussed in this chapter to help me to modify those behaviors.
- I will determine whether I exhibit any of the people-pleasing behaviors, and if so, I will use the steps discussed in this chapter to modify those behaviors.
- I will learn how to determine which situations provoke or trigger anger in me.
- I will learn how to use disputing self-talk to help reduce my anger and stress.
- I will learn how to eliminate free-floating hostility.
- I will practice assertive (not aggressive or nonassertive) behaviors.

Melanie is a financial planner with many demanding clients. She has always been on the anxious side, both in her job and in her life in general. Impatient in lines and in congested traffic, she frequently gets so frustrated that she can feel her blood pressure escalate. Speaking rapidly, she finds herself finishing sentences for people because they are just too slow for her.

Since college, she often finds herself thinking about two or more things at the same time and thrives on multitasking. On the phone with clients, she pretends to be listening, but often runs through her email or looks at message slips her assistant places on her desk. Because Melanie considers wasting time almost a sin, she brushes her teeth while showering and always brings reading material with her to the restroom. The idea of relaxation is foreign to her. She believes that if she does take time just for herself, she will fail to accomplish her goals (recall the "all-or-nothing" thinking pattern).

Melanie's goals are lofty; they include being honored as her firm's number one fee producer for the year. This competitive nature fuels free-floating hostility, which she doesn't even realize is part of her personality. Her hostility surfaces when anyone or anything gets in the way of what she is trying to accomplish. Colleagues at her firm accuse her of making "20 dollar reactions to 20 cent provocations." She is sometimes abrasive and downright rude to her colleagues when she is stressed.

Melanie has a pervasive need to control everything in her life, including her clients. Therefore, when a client asks her a difficult question or wants her to explain why a recommended product isn't doing well, Melanie views this as a challenge to her need for control. Her irritable reactions in such circumstances have resulted in several clients complaining to her that they don't feel valued by her. They protested that they felt as if they were imposing on her, that she wasn't listening to them, and that she was rushing them off the phone. She brushed off those comments with made-up excuses, such as "I was having a difficult day because I wasn't feeling well." She has also used sarcasm and inappropriate humor, both of which were at the expense of her colleagues during staff meetings.

Now let's examine another advisor, Tom. Tom is a people pleaser. He avoids all confrontations and has trouble committing to recommendations when challenged by his clients. He seems to modify his suggestions based on their reactions, rather than on what he really believes is in their best interest.

Always showing up on time is of paramount importance to him because he doesn't want to disappoint anyone. Tom is one of the most well-liked advisors in his firm. He has a wonderful family and many friends. Everyone who knows Tom comments on what a nice person he is. However, he lost two clients because they complained that when they asked for his advice, he was not definitive and came across as wishy-washy, and they felt that they were making their own decisions with which Tom simply went along.

Tom's people-pleasing behaviors began to take a toll on his body. He missed many days at the office because of vague symptoms that his doctors couldn't diagnose, let alone cure. Of course, this worried him even more, and his stress level continued to rise. Eventually, he developed chronic stomach problems that his doctor labeled "irritable bowel syndrome," a very painful malady due in large part to not expressing emotions. These symptoms are also common with nonassertive people.

We will discover what happened to both Melanie and Tom at the end of the chapter.

TWO PERSONALITY TYPES THAT PROMOTE STRESS

The condition you are in right now largely depends upon what you have been thinking and doing to and for yourself—all your life ... You are the sum total of all the causes and effects you have set up in yourself through your mental and emotional attitudes.

—BRISTOL AND SHERMAN (1987)

If you recognize in yourself several of the traits typical for the two personality types described in this chapter, you need not worry. The important point in the previous quote is that it is our *thinking patterns* and habits, *not* our personality traits, per se, that determine our destiny and how we react to provocations. Whether we set off our fight-or-flight response—our sympathetic nervous system (SNS)—is really up to us. Because we are certainly capable of modifying and controlling our thoughts and behaviors, we don't have to become prisoners of our genetic hardwiring. But let's explore two common types of genetic hardwiring that can potentially fuel stress, if we don't recognize these traits and modify them.

Melanie and Tom display two very different personality types, yet both sets of traits can potentially tax their internal balance (homeostasis), even putting their physical and emotional health at risk. Again, having either one of these personalities (or for that matter, a combination of the two) is not necessarily unfortunate. What would be unfortunate is failing to modify those behaviors that are harmful—emotionally, behaviorally, or physically.

Melanie's personality constellation fits the well-known pattern described as *Type-A personality*. The discovery and labeling of Type-A personality by two cardiologists is a fascinating story. Meyer Friedman and Ray Rosenman (1974) were running a successful practice when their office manager brought to their attention the need to reupholster the waiting room chairs. It seems that only a few inches of the seats (toward the front edge) and the armrests of most of the chairs were worn through. The remainder of each chair was intact.

Subsequent observations of the patients in the waiting room showed that the majority of them sat on the edges of their seats, impatiently fidgeting and rubbing their hands nervously across the armrests while waiting to be called in to the examination rooms. In contrast, worn chairs were not found in the waiting rooms of other specialists, including neurologists, urologists, or oncologists; therefore, it was concluded that there must be something different about people with coronary heart disease (CHD). Accordingly, this led to a host of research studies showing the relationship between these personality traits and the onset of CHD.

One of the hallmarks of Seyle's (1976) remarkable work in the field of stress was the observation that the body needs frequent periods of quiet and calm to replenish and refresh itself. Type-A people rarely allow themselves periods of worry-free relaxation. Table 4.1 is a summary of the major traits that make up the Type-A pattern of behaviors and emotions.

 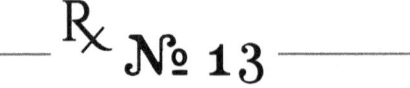

Review Table 4.1, Checklist of Potential Type-A Behaviors, to see if you fit this profile.

It's important to understand that Type-A folks come with a wide variety of trait combinations, and you don't need to have all of them to fit the Type-A pattern. Check off those that apply to you.

Good News!

Regardless of your genetically wired personality traits, you can learn to avoid switching on the SNS, which is ultimately how to control your stress.

Among all of the behaviors represented by Type-A people, the one shown in Friedman and Rosenman's (1974) original research to be most predictive of heart disease was *free-floating hostility*. Studies of a variety of occupations consistently show that having a high level of hostility predicts heart disease, hardening of the arteries, and higher death rates from these diseases, as well as higher death rates from *all* diseases.

Table 4.1	CHECKLIST OF POTENTIAL TYPE-A BEHAVIORS

Check any that apply to you.

- *Sense of Time Urgency*
  - ☐ Blinks rapidly
  - ☐ Cuts others off in traffic
  - ☐ Cuts others off before they finish their sentences ("uh huh ... I know, I know")
  - ☐ Hates lines and waiting
  - ☐ Is impatient
  - ☐ Multitasks to save time and to avoid forgetting anything
  - ☐ Needs to achieve more and more in less and less time
  - ☐ Speaks rapidly
- *All-or-Nothing Thinking*
  - ☐ Thinks in black or white, perfect or failure extremes
- *Work Addiction*
  - ☐ Engages in multitasking (e.g., brushes teeth while showering, reads stock reports while watching TV, dictates memos into the phone while driving the car)
  - ☐ Has trouble delegating
  - ☐ Needs to be successful
- *Free-Floating Hostility*
  - ☐ Appears insensitive to others' feelings
  - ☐ Clenches fists during ordinary conversation
  - ☐ Grinds teeth during sleep—facial expressions show hostility, jaw and mouth muscle tightness (jaw pain near hairline is referred to as TMJ pain)
  - ☐ Has difficulty expressing love and feelings, except with pets
  - ☐ Is extremely competitive—wanting to win at all costs, whether it is an important or simple game (e.g., golf)
  - ☐ Is easily irritated
  - ☐ Maintains an intimidating style
  - ☐ Raises voice frequently
  - ☐ Uses sarcasm, abrasiveness, and humor at others' expense

(continued)

| Table 4.1 | CHECKLIST OF POTENTIAL TYPE-A BEHAVIORS (CONT.) |

- ❖ *Inadequate Self-Esteem (usually unaware of this)*
  - ☐ Displays signs of insecurity, which lies at the core of the need to prove self over and over, thus the time pressure and inability to relax
  - ☐ Has expectations that exceed perceived achievements
  - ☐ Micromanages for fear of failing
- ❖ *Unconscious Drive Toward Self-Destruction*
  - ☐ Displays self-destructive behaviors, including alcohol, tobacco, and drug use to deal with anxiety
  - ☐ Experiences vague pains and headaches often
  - ☐ Is prone to ulcers and heart attacks
- ❖ *Need to Be in Control at All Times*
  - ☐ Prefers to drive, rather than be a passenger, in order to keep sense of control
  - ☐ Makes all decisions for clients, spouse, children, and even employees without giving them an opportunity

Good News!

Regardless of the number of Type-A traits you possess, you can learn to reduce the hostility component, and once you do that, you dramatically reduce the risk of heart disease.

℞ № 14

Simplify your life. Ask yourself what really needs to be done. If you don't perform a specific task right now, what's the worst that will happen? Get a good spam blocker so you can avoid having to read the bulk of your e-mails, and be selective regarding the number of people to whom you give your e-mail address. Read Lakein's *How to Get Control of Your Time and Your Life* (1973).

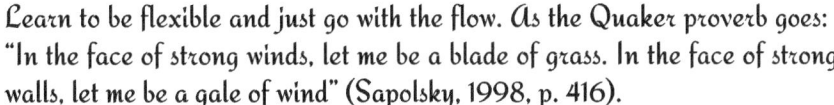

R̞ № 15

Learn to be flexible and just go with the flow. As the Quaker proverb goes: "In the face of strong winds, let me be a blade of grass. In the face of strong walls, let me be a gale of wind" (Sapolsky, 1998, p. 416).

Tom's personality constellation is very different, but it's just as stressful and harmful to his emotional and physical health. Tom's personality structure fits closely with what has been termed the *people-pleasing personality*, and he pays a big price for maintaining some of his traits. A person with this pattern of traits exhibits the behavioral tendencies listed in Table 4.2.

Table 4.2   CHECKLIST OF POTENTIAL PEOPLE-PLEASING BEHAVIORS

Check any that apply to you.

❖ *Desires and Needs Everyone's Approval*

- ☐ Is vulnerable to being manipulated and taken advantage of because of the strong desire to be liked
- ☐ Rarely pleased or satisfied with self
- ☐ Will risk an accident rather than be late for an event, imagining *What will they think of me if I'm late?*

Avoids Confrontations—Not Assertive

- ☐ Agrees with others and goes with the flow, rather than challenge anyone
- ☐ Has difficulty returning items to stores
- ☐ Has difficulty sending food back in restaurants
- ☐ Rationalizes nonassertive reactions to incidents (e.g., *It wasn't the waiter's fault that the food wasn't cooked correctly, so I didn't want to upset him by sending back my food.*)
- ☐ Feels guilty turning people down for favors

(continued)

Table 4.2	CHECKLIST OF POTENTIAL PEOPLE-PLEASING BEHAVIORS (CONT.)

- ❖ *Avoids Expressing Criticism—Not Assertive*
    - ☐ Is hesitant to say no to people
    - ☐ Is hesitant to show anger and disappointment, even when it is justified (sometimes avoids showing anger because of fear of exploding)
    - ☐ Wants to be seen by others as nice and believes that disagreeing or expressing self assertively equates to not being nice
- ❖ *Suffers From Self-Doubt, Insecurity, and Fear*
    - ☐ Afraid of making decisions (to avoid mistakes) and seeks the advice of others, rather than trusting own judgment
    - ☐ Avoids conflict at all costs, thus playing a charade in relationships
    - ☐ Believes that pleasing others and being seen as nice will avoid negative feedback
    - ☐ Doesn't risk being real and expressing negative emotions
    - ☐ Fears rejection, abandonment, conflict, and loneliness
    - ☐ Has problems in relationships because of rarely giving feedback to others about what behavior is offensive or hurtful
    - ☐ Misjudges others' behavior as being "mad at me"
    - ☐ Second-guesses self constantly
    - ☐ Self-doubt and fear remain because the person doesn't risk being "real" with others
- ❖ *Stuffs negative emotions down, ignoring them*
    - ☐ Vulnerable to *implosions*—the body pays the price of not expressing negative emotions
    - ☐ Examples of physiological and psychological consequences of repressed emotions are migraines, gastrointestinal problems, back pain, chronic-fatigue syndrome, depression, anxiety, hostility, and alcohol and substance abuse

People pleasers are often vulnerable to being taken advantage of and manipulated. Moreover, they are hurting themselves by avoiding negative emotions at all costs. The most common chronic problems for people pleasers are sadness and internal physical upheaval.

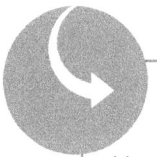

Good News!

You are a prisoner of neither your genetics, nor your upbringing. Once you recognize your self-defeating, emotionally inappropriate thinking patterns, you can begin to change in a very healthy way, regardless of the personality traits you have exhibited all your life.

Many research findings connect specific personality traits of financial advisors to physiological stress outcomes (e.g., Cass, Shaw & LeBlanc, 2008). Anxious advisors have exaggerated stress responses to the task of reaching out to potential and existing clients, with neck muscle tension predominating. More socially comfortable extroverts, on the other hand, seem to have effective coping responses to the same tasks and suffer less stress.

Non-competitive, more timid advisors who habitually think about being in uncomfortable situations in their role as advisors are the most prone to feeling inadequate and lack coping skills.

UNDERSTANDING THE REAL CAUSES OF YOUR STRESS

If you have Type-A or people-pleasing personality characteristics or any of the other traits described earlier, fear not. Next, you will find methods of modifying *any* behaviors that make you more prone to stress.

YOU CAN START MODIFYING SOME OF YOUR TYPE-A BEHAVIORS TODAY!

> *Type-A behavior—however induced and however deep-seated—can be changed by the individual himself or herself, and we have proved it.*
>
> —MEYER FRIEDMAN AND NANCY ULMER (1984)

The next time you feel any negative emotion, revisit Table 4.1 to see if you are engaging in these behaviors. Then, use the information in this chapter to modify these behaviors.

Allow me to reiterate that if you are a Type-A person, you don't need to change your whole personality, which you couldn't do even if you wanted to. However, there is much research, cited by Friedman and Rosenman (1974) and Roskies (1987), showing that Type-A folks typically respond to stress in ways that lead to CHD. When discussing the reasons for increased CHD in Type-A people, Roskies (1987) notes the following:

> In response to certain types of challenge and threat, Type-A people tend to show greater elevations in blood pressure, heart rate, cortisol, epinephrine, and norepinephrine than Type Bs ... Episodic elevations in blood pressure and heart rate are thought to damage the inner layer of the coronary arteries, thereby contributing to atherosclerosis and subsequent CHD. (p. 20)

Type-A people possess many wonderful characteristics, including creativity, drive, persistence, and attention to detail. In fact, Friedman and Ulmer (1984) cite a study in which they determined that large percentages of Type-A people were found in a variety of respected professions, including the following:

- $ University presidents
- $ Bank presidents
- $ Corporation chairpersons
- $ Generals and admirals
- $ Archbishops, bishops, and rabbis
- $ Nobel laureates
- $ Congressmen and senators
- $ Federal judges

Actually, we find successful Type-A people in virtually all of the professions, including medicine, law, engineering—and yes, especially in the financial advising profession. However, Friedman and Ulmer (1984) are quick to point out large percentages of people they labeled *Type-B*, who also are successful in these professions. In other words, you don't need to hold onto harmful Type-A traits in order to maintain your success! If you are a Type-A person, it's not your time urgency, impatience, hostility, or need to be in control that makes you a success. In fact, those traits are usually counterproductive to success. Friedman and Ulmer suggest that your success is more likely because of your creativity, decision making, confidence, organizational skills, and drive to accomplish your goals.

Type-B people, in general, don't have a sense of time urgency, don't give themselves time to contemplate, relax, and "recharge their batteries," don't feel good about themselves and maintain good self-esteem, don't get irritated with the inadequacies of their subordinates, don't demonstrate free-floating hostility, and are usually able to cope with stress quite effectively.

A common objection raised by Type-A people when it is suggested that they consider changing some of their behaviors is "I was born this way," "my father (or mother) is this way," or "I can't become a different person." The intent is never to change your personality. Many of our behavioral habits feel like they are part of our personalities because we have always acted that way, but our self-talk and behavioral habits are *learned* over time. This is very important to know because anything that is learned can be unlearned. Modifying habits or learning new ones does not mean a complete makeover; you can choose to *modify* those behaviors and habits that are working against you, without having to become a completely different person.

Another objection often raised by Type-A people is: "I don't want to mess with success. I'm happy being a Type-A person. It's worked for me up until now, so why should I change?" The answer to this objection is that once you modify those behaviors and habits that are potentially harmful, you will continue to work with the same enthusiasm, creativity, and zeal, but without the stress that so often accompanies your work.

So let's talk about modifying behaviors and habits. In Chapter 3, I discussed how we tend to *awfulize* to ourselves when we face situations that we interpret negatively, resulting in painful emotions. These unfortunate ways of thinking persist because we are creatures of habit. But, as you now understand, our thinking patterns can certainly be challenged and changed.

In Chapter 1, I referenced research that shows that 75 to 90 percent of all illnesses and physical symptoms are stress related (AIS, n.d.), and Dr. Helmstetter (1982) describes research stating that up to 75 percent of our thoughts are negative and counterproductive, ultimately contributing to the onset or exacerbation of many of these unwanted physical and emotional outcomes. As you now know, once you recognize your negative thinking patterns, you *can* change them.

It follows, then, that once you recognize and understand your Type-A behaviors, and realize that modifying these behaviors, feelings, and attitudes is *under your control,* you can actually make changes that will make a *real difference* in your life and health. Several practical prescriptions follow for behaviors you can build into your daily routine to modify Type-A components.

Rx № 17

Become aware of the triggers to your stress feelings.

You can easily identify the daily hassles in and out of the office that trigger stress feelings. Is it dealing with a particular client, your manager monitoring your cold calls, trying to save time for your family, or something else? Using the checklist in Table 4.3, you can list all of the specific triggers you are aware of and rate the level of tension you feel with each—either mild, moderate, or high.

Rx № 18

Find a relaxation technique you're comfortable with and make it part of your daily routine. See Appendix C for a relaxation example. Practice your relaxation skills in a place where you will be left alone and not interrupted by the phone, TV, or other people.

Besides the method described in Appendix C, you can use any relaxation routine you are comfortable with, including yoga, meditation, and even self-hypnosis. If you use the technique in Appendix C, you simply read the words slowly into a recorder, and then play the recording back for yourself frequently. The recording will only be 12 to 15 minutes long, so it won't take much of your time, but it will be a powerful tool for you if you make a habit of listening to it. The best time to practice relaxation is either before you go to work or as soon as you get home. Try to develop the habit of practicing daily, perhaps rotating different techniques so you don't get bored with a single method.

4 | How to Thrive Despite Stress-Prone Personality Traits

Table 4.3 — CHECKLIST OF POTENTIAL STRESS TRIGGERS AND THE LEVEL OF TENSION GENERATED BY EACH

Check all that apply to you, and add other triggers you are aware of. Check the tension level of mild, moderate, or high for each trigger.

Stress Triggers	Level of Stress / Tension		
Business Related + Off the Job	*Mild*	*Moderate*	*High*
☐ Dealing with a difficult client's personality and/or behavior			
☐ My manager asking to meet with me			
☐ My children complaining that they don't get to see me enough			
☐ Deadlines for completing paperwork			
☐ Explaining complex details about a product to a client who doesn't follow me			
☐ Dealing with long lines during my lunch break			
☐ Receiving negative feedback from my mentor			
☐ Traffic to and from the office			
☐ Not making enough money			
☐ Pressure to get referrals			
☐ Dealing with my teenager's issues			
☐ Taking a vacation without feeling guilty			

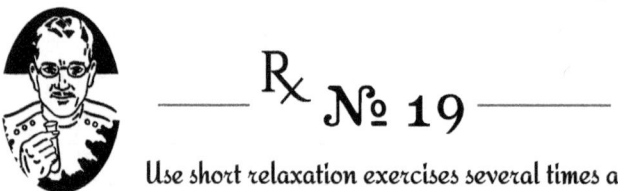

Rx № 19

Use short relaxation exercises several times a day.

Besides the 12- to 15-minute relaxation technique you employ each day, you can use an abbreviated version (1–2 minutes) several times a day. Choose parts of the exercise that work fastest for you from the longer session found in Appendix C. For example, if you enjoy the muscle tensing and releasing routine, you can use an abbreviated muscle tensing and releasing program to prepare yourself for a potentially tension-producing situation, such as your boss wanting to meet with you an hour from now.

A minute of deep breathing and muscle tensing and releasing can go a long way toward relaxing you in advance. If you enjoy imagining a relaxing scene, take some deep, relaxing breaths and go to the scene for a minute or two.

You can also use either of these shortened versions as a first step in regaining self-control whenever you find yourself in a state of high tension.

Rx № 20

Get in touch with your false beliefs and change them.

These are beliefs that may underlie your issues with impatience and time urgency. For example, you may believe that your diligence directed at always being on time has helped you become successful in your advising career. It's almost as if someone told you that it's your impatience and irritation that has made you such a wonderful advisor! This false belief comes from not understanding the real reasons you are successful, such as your intelligence, creativity, persistence, motivation, and ability to help your clients create portfolios that particularly address their needs—*not* because you are impatient and compulsive about getting all of your work done before spending time relaxing or being with your family. In fact, you would undoubtedly be even *more* successful if you recharged your batteries with relaxing breaks several times each day.

Getting in touch with false beliefs also means understanding the irrational self-talk that is involved in each situation and challenging (rebutting) that talk. Table 4.4 on the next page provides examples and spaces for you to enter stress-provoking situations that occur in your life.

Second, rate the tension level (C) you feel in the next column. This is the combination of the provocation and the resultant critical self-talk (B) that sets off (triggers) that tension. The critical final step is providing yourself with rational, disputing (rebuttal) self-talk (D). Write down as many rebuttal thoughts as you can think of in the box on the far right.

Once you see that your rebuttal thoughts make much more sense and are much more logical than your original thoughts, your tension level should reduce dramatically. This is the ultimate result of rationally re-thinking your situation. By writing down these provoking situations whenever you are aware of them, noting your self-talk and especially your *rebuttal* self-talk, you will ultimately develop the habit of engaging in positive, rational thinking whenever you have a provocative situation, resulting in keeping your stress and tension levels manageable.

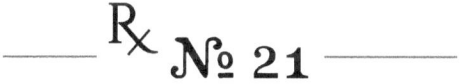

℞ № 21

Recognize the price you are paying to achieve more and more in less and less time.

When the underlying goal is to achieve more and more, the downside is that you are preoccupied with your own activities and ignoring the needs of the people around you. Think about the time your spouse, children, and friends are missing because of this unfortunate habit. So start taking an interest in the lives of those around you. *Take the time to listen to them,* and show them that they are important to you. (See also Stress Mastery Prescription 29.)

Table 4.4 Stress Provocations, Tension Level, Critical Self-Talk Triggers, and Disputed Self-Talk

Here are examples of how to fill in this table whenever you are stressed. Add other examples from your own experience.

Provocative Situation (A)	Tension Level (C)	Critical Self-Talk (Trigger) (B)	Disputed Self-Talk (Rebuttal) (D)
1. My most challenging client is insisting on an immediate meeting with me.	High	1. I hate this man. He's making my life miserable. I feel completely helpless and can't control his panic whenever the markets slide. He will always make my life miserable. I feel helpless.	1. I don't have to be perfect and be able to control every single client I have. I will bring this case up in a staff meeting and get my colleagues' input about how to handle such a client. If no one has any good ideas, I'll make arrangements to transfer this client out of my practice. (see Chapter 7)
2. My manager has asked to meet with me at the end of the day.	High	2. What now? I'm tired of his criticism, and I believe he's trying to push me out of the practice.	2. I don't know for sure that he's calling me in to criticize me. I'll just see what happens, and if there's criticism, I'll assert myself as I've been practicing. I have no evidence to conclude that he wants me out of the practice.
3. I can't stand the traffic to and from the office.	Moderate	3. I have to leave home early to get to the office on time, and I'm exhausted by the time I get home.	3. I know I have no control over the traffic. I can practice my relaxation skills while driving and can bring calming and comforting CDs to play while the traffic is stalled. I can also prepare snacks to bring with me on the way home to energize me after the long work day.
4. My spouse and children demand too much of my time.	Moderate	4. They just don't understand how drained I am when I get home, and then I have to do research to prepare for meetings the next day. I just can't be pulled in any more directions!	4. My spouse and children love me, and I'm a very important part of their lives. I will budget my time to allow for some special time for each of them, without feeling guilty about taking time away from my job requirements.

Table 4.4 Stress Provocations, Tension Level, Critical Self-Talk Triggers, and Disputed Self-Talk (Blank)

Make copies of this table before you fill it in so that you will have tables to fill in every time you feel stressed.

Provocative Situation (A)	Tension Level (C)	Critical Self-Talk (Trigger) (B)	Disputed Self-Talk (Rebuttal) (D)
1.			
2.			
3.			
4.			

Adapted from Matthew McKay and Martha Davis. *Thoughts and Feelings.* 1981, with permission from Harbinger Press.

℞ № 22

Get a time-management book, and practice the techniques you learn from it.

♦ ♦ ♦

An even better idea is to take a time-management course. Get rid of the relatively unimportant minutiae that fill your weekly schedule and prioritize relaxation, family time, and reading into your weekly schedule. Examine your routines, and objectively determine which ones you can let go of without disastrous effects. This also addresses the important issue of balancing your career and your life. Recognize how balancing your career with your family or off-the-job interests will help you succeed in the long run because the off-the-job activities will make you whole. Go ahead and *take a risk* by spending relaxing time with family, friends, and yourself each week, without allowing work to interfere and without feeling guilty in the process. You'll soon realize how much *more productive* you will be in your career.

Here are additional tips:

℞ № 23

Never skip or shorten breakfast.

♦ ♦ ♦

Nutritionists point out the critical value of eating a good breakfast. Don't make this the hurried beginning to a hurried day. Enjoy it with family members, and model the appropriate breakfast behavior for your children. Make sure it's a nutritious breakfast, such as including a protein shake, which doesn't take long to prepare.

Take multiple mini-breaks during the day.

Break up your work routine by taking the time to go for a walk, meditate, or listen to soothing music or your relaxation routine on your iPod, smart phone, iPad, or portable CD player.

What you gain by recharging your batteries in this way will be far more beneficial for you than utilizing the 10 minutes or so for work purposes.

№ 26

Make a deal with yourself that you will never leave the office later than 6:00 p.m. (unless you have a meeting scheduled).

Clean off your desk each evening so that you are greeted in the morning by a clean one. It increases stress to come into the office and find a pile of work that you must dive into. Give yourself a break. Pressuring yourself to keep working is literally increasing the chances of the onset of diseases, which will ultimately cost you much more time.

℞ № 27

Each day, make a deal with yourself to accomplish one task at a time, rather than overwhelming yourself with multiple tasks.

Do one activity at a time instead of cramming everything in at once. *Listen* to what colleagues and clients are saying to you without simultaneously thinking about other things you need to get done. Get used to focusing your complete attention on one task at a time.

If you're worried that you'll forget to do something, get a pad of paper at the nearest print shop that says, "Things to Do Today" across the top of each sheet. Have a box next to each line you write on so you can have fun checking off each item once you complete it. This will ensure that you won't forget anything so you can do one thing at a time without fear of forgetting.

℞ № 28

Pay attention to your angry and hostile behaviors, and learn to modify them using anger-mastery techniques.

Now you know that the free-floating hostility component of many Type-A people's personalities is the most dangerous risk factor for CHD. Although anger-mastery techniques are beyond the scope of this book, there are many excellent books that cover this important subject, including my favorite, *The Anger Control Workbook* (McKay and Rogers, 1985). In addition, I have a hypnotic anger-mastery CD series available for this purpose (Singer, 2009).

Here is a tip to get you started: *Get an objective handle on when and how you react with anger and hostility.* Ask your spouse, colleagues, and friends to be honest with you and tell you when you act angry or hostile. Ask them to be as specific as possible so you will understand exactly how they see you, even though you may not see these behaviors in yourself. Just as with stress, it's crucial to understand the self-talk triggers that set off your anger.

As you can see in Table 4.5, you can examine each situation in which you feel anger and frustration (A), determine the self-talk that triggered you (B), and dispute (rebuttal) that self-talk (D) to reduce your hostile emotional and behavioral responses to the situation (C1 and C2), which are not included in this table. The ultimate outcomes (E) when you engage in such disputed self-talk (rebuttals) are healthy stress-reducing consequences.

Table 4.5 — ANGER PROVOCATIONS, CRITICAL SELF-TALK TRIGGERS, DISPUTED SELF-TALK, AND ULTIMATE OUTCOMES

Examples of how to fill in this table whenever you are angry.

Provocative Situation (A)	Critical Self-Talk (Trigger) (B)	Disputed Self-Talk (Rebuttal) (D)	Ultimate Outcomes (E)
1. My manager wants to come into my office to listen to how I handle cold calls.	1. *This isn't fair. I'll feel very nervous being observed and judged by my manager. I'm really angry about this.*	1. *He's just doing his job. He isn't trying to see me screw up or get me upset. He really hopes I do well. My job is to keep practicing and with his input, I will master the art of cold calling/prospecting. I can also read an excellent book to help me overcome my fears of cold calling (Dudley & Goodson, 2007).*	1. Once I started to talk to myself rationally and to practice prospecting/cold calling with the input of my manager, I started to do really well and my anger went away.

(continued)

Table 4.5	ANGER PROVOCATIONS, CRITICAL SELF-TALK TRIGGERS, DISPUTED SELF-TALK, AND ULTIMATE OUTCOMES (CONT.)		
Provocative Situation (A)	**Critical Self-Talk (Trigger) (B)**	**Disputed Self-Talk (Rebuttal) (D)**	**Ultimate Outcomes (E)**
2. I have a high-value client who loves to challenge my suggestions and make me uncomfortable. My anger at him spills over to my being angry at other people in the office.	2. *This client has absolutely no respect for me and enjoys embarrassing me. I get angry every time I have to speak with him. I wish I could get rid of him, but he brings a lot of income into my practice.*	2. *I need to be assertive with this client and explain how difficult it is to make progress in my planning if he's going to challenge every suggestion I make. Therefore, I'll offer to refer him elsewhere, or if he isn't ok with that, I'll write him a letter of termination. Having him out of my practice will decrease my stress level tremendously, and I'll make up the financial loss elsewhere.* (see Chapter 7)	2. I was able to get this client out of my practice, reducing my stress level and angry feelings dramatically. My assistant tells me that since I got this client out of my practice, I'm much more pleasant and less moody. I'm now much more motivated to attract new business because of my better mood and demeanor.

Adapted from Matthew McKay and Martha Davis. *Thoughts and Feelings.* 1981, with permission from Harbinger Press.

| Table 4.5 | ANGER PROVOCATIONS, CRITICAL SELF-TALK TRIGGERS, DISPUTED SELF-TALK, AND ULTIMATE OUTCOMES (BLANK) |

Make copies of this table before you fill it in so that you will have tables to fill in every time you feel angry.

Provocative Situation (A)	Critical Self-Talk (Trigger) (B)	Disputed Self-Talk (Rebuttal) (D)	Ultimate Outcomes (E)
1.			
2.			
3.			

Again, it's very important to recognize the statements you are saying to yourself when you are feeling angry or frustrated. Then, give yourself more calming, peaceful, rational rebuttals, and your anger should be reduced dramatically. Practice writing down situations that provoke your anger and frustration each day in Table 4.5, under Provocative Situation (A), then record your self-talk triggers and disputed self-talk. This will eventually lead to positive, rational thinking that should really help prevent or remediate your angry emotions.

Even though it may be embarrassing, it will help to share this list of anger-provoking situations with your spouse or good friend because that person will be able to give you an objective view of the situation. Hopefully, this will help you see when you tend to overreact.

You now know about *free-floating hostility*. This is continual anger and irritability without a specific cause or provocation, expressed frequently—even in trivial situations—and often in subtle ways, such as through sarcasm or humor at others' expense. Tips for eliminating this free-floating hostility are contained in Table 4.6.

Table 4.6 TEN TIPS FOR ELIMINATING FREE-FLOATING HOSTILITY

Check all that apply to you.

- ☐ Tell your spouse, colleagues, and friends that you realize you are carrying around free-floating hostility and that you plan to eliminate it. (This will help you commit to it, just like announcing a weight-loss goal. Have a prearranged signal for them to give you when they notice you are getting hot under the collar.)

- ☐ Regularly express appreciation to these people for helping you to recognize and manage these emotions.

- ☐ Regularly express love and affection to your spouse and children, and freely express to your friends and colleagues how much you value them.

- ☐ Surprise one of these people at least once a month with tickets to a movie, concert, or the like. Your spouse was once your sweetheart. Start treating her or him like that again.

- ☐ Examine the opinions of people with whom you disagree, from their perspective, before judging them.

- ☐ When playing games for fun with your spouse and children, stop being so competitive, and try to allow them to experience the joy of winning.

- ☐ Look in a mirror several times a day to see if your face exhibits anger, frustration, or irritation. Practice smiling in the mirror, and memorize the muscles in your laughing face so you can display it during the day. (See if your forehead is wrinkled and your eyebrows are turned down and look for muscle tension. Then get into the habit of smiling more.)

- ☐ Go to sporting events, where it's socially acceptable to yell and scream your guts out! (Get it out of your system.)

- ☐ Each evening ask yourself what you did to show kindness to someone.

- ☐ Deliberately admit that you're wrong in as many situations as you can, and write the situations down.

℞ № 29

Take a course in Active Listening. Begin practicing this technique at home, and once you are comfortable with it, use it with your clients.

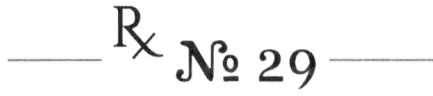

HOW TO USE ACTIVE-LISTENING SKILLS

One of the problems that many Type-A people have is that they do not really listen to people with whom they are communicating. Their minds are filled with other agendas, and they have a tendency to want to control the dialogue, rather than have an open exchange. *Active listening* means being patient and paying close attention to the messages people are communicating to you. Because Type-A people are so often impatient, they frequently finish others' sentences for them, as if they are saying to themselves, *I get it, so you don't have to finish.* This leads to projecting their own ideas onto the communicator and into the message, thus incorrectly assuming its intent.

Here is a model for practicing active-listening skills:

- **Ask gentle questions to understand what the speaker is trying to say and the emotions involved.**

  For example, you could ask: "Are you angry because you don't think I took your ideas into consideration before making my decision?"

- **Reflect back or paraphrase what you heard before responding or commenting on it.**

  If you were not listening carefully to the meaning, the speaker will clarify your paraphrase. It's important not to respond until they agree that your interpretation of what they were saying is correct.

- **When you are listening, don't be doing other things, such as shuffling papers.**

  Always maintain eye contact with the speaker and sit on the same level, rather than one of you standing while the other sits.

- **Watch for nonverbal behavior (body language, facial expressions).**

  Scientific research shows that body language, expressions, and tone of voice will often give you more information about the message than words. In terms of your own body language, when you are listening, lean forward toward the speaker, breathing easily and remaining relaxed. Tenseness and frowning on your part suggest that you are angry, frustrated, or impatient with the speaker.

- **Acknowledge the message you are hearing; you don't have to agree—just acknowledge what you hear the speaker saying.**

  Put yourself in the shoes of the other speaker and try to see where he is coming from, even if you don't agree. Just listen and understand. A nod here and there also communicates that you are listening; however, it may also indicate to the speaker that you agree with what is being said, so be selective with your nods.

- **Don't feel pressed to have an answer.**

  Tell the speaker you'll think about what she is asking and get back with her the next day, for example. Avoid your tendency to be impatient and rush an answer that you may later regret.

§ **Always allow the speaker to finish.**

You may need to take notes if the speaker is long winded, but be patient rather than interrupt, roll your eyes, or get frustrated.

YOU CAN START MODIFYING SOME OF YOUR PEOPLE-PLEASING BEHAVIORS TODAY!

You can stop the progression of the disease to please, and you can change now.

—HARRIET BRAIKER (1995)

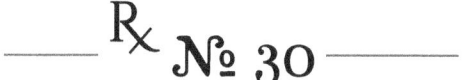

Review the people-pleasing behaviors in Table 4.2 to see if you fit this profile.

Table 4.7 lists the specific beliefs that underlie people-pleasing behaviors. As you can imagine, maintaining such beliefs makes it difficult to risk changing behaviors. For example, believing that you must avoid confrontations at all costs will prevent you from standing up for yourself in many situations.

You can see that these beliefs are self-defeating. You need to understand that the reason people like you is *not* because you always say yes; you are a good person, and they like you because of your values, not because you always accommodate them.

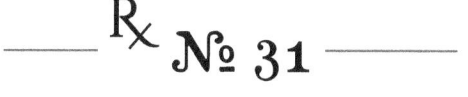

Learn how to assert yourself without feeling guilty.

Table 4.7	CHECKLIST OF 10 COMMON PEOPLE-PLEASING BELIEFS

Check all that apply to you.

- ☐ I need to be adored by everyone.
- ☐ I need to avoid confrontations at all costs.
- ☐ I should never have negative feelings or emotions regarding anyone in my life.
- ☐ I believe that others should treat me the way I treat them.
- ☐ I believe that if I don't disappoint people, they shouldn't criticize or reject me.
- ☐ I believe that because I am so nice to others, they should never hurt me, be angry with me, or treat me unfairly.
- ☐ I should strive to always do what others want, expect, or need from me, even if it hurts me in the process.
- ☐ Putting others' feelings ahead of mine makes me a good person.
- ☐ I should never say no to people or disappoint them.
- ☐ There is a reward waiting for me in heaven for being such a nice person to everyone and putting them first, ahead of me.

How to Assert Yourself

Most of the time, we communicate with others in one of three ways: aggressively, nonassertively, or assertively. For the Type-A person, aggressive communication is common; for the people pleaser, nonassertive communication is the predominant method.

Nonassertive responses involve not sharing your true feelings and trying to accommodate others' requests or agree with their point of view, regardless of how you *really* feel. These responses reflect weakness and the belief that you don't have the right, power, or ability to stand up for yourself.

Nonassertive people are often apologetic when they ask for something and frequently sprinkle their language with self-deprecating comments, such as, "This is probably a stupid idea, but…" They also avoid beginning a sentence with the word "I" and prefer to deflect attention from their feelings and emotions. On the other hand, *aggressive* responses involve trying to overpower the other person, proving you are right, regardless of whether you are insulting or embarrassing the other person.

4 | How to Thrive Despite Stress-Prone Personality Traits

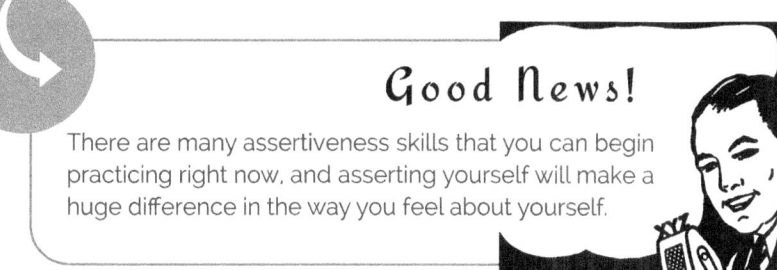

Good News!
There are many assertiveness skills that you can begin practicing right now, and asserting yourself will make a huge difference in the way you feel about yourself.

Assertive responses are based on an attitude that *you* are just as entitled to express your true feelings as anyone with whom you are communicating. Assertiveness means being open and direct about how you feel, without feeling anxiety or guilt. Many nonassertive people feel uncomfortable even giving compliments and positive feedback to others, so assertiveness involves being able to express *all* emotions without discomfort.

But being assertive also means that you have the freedom to choose whether assertive behavior is appropriate in a particular situation. There may be times when it is not in your best interest to assert yourself. For example, if your manager arrived at the office very upset about what happened at home, that may not be the appropriate time to assert yourself in criticizing a decision he made about you the day before. Common sense dictates using all of the information at hand when deciding when and where to assert yourself. The key is to know that you made a rational decision to delay your request, rather than delaying it simply because you were uncomfortable asserting yourself.

Maintaining the people-pleasing behavior of nonassertiveness can take as big a toll on your emotional and physical well-being as do many Type-A traits. Table 4.8 points out the dangers of maintaining these beliefs.

Table 4.8 DANGERS INHERENT IN PEOPLE-PLEASING BELIEFS

- ❖ Review Chapter 3. You will quickly recognize that all of these beliefs are examples of illogical, distorted thinking, including "should" statements, mind reading, fortune-telling, emotional reasoning, labeling, and overgeneralizing. With distorted thinking, you set yourself up for disappointment, confusion, and self-blame when you don't get the results you desire.

- ❖ Because these beliefs and denials of reality force you to swallow negative emotions, thoughts, and behaviors (or at least not show them to others), you cause implosions inside your body, leading to illnesses, a compromised immune system, and emotional distress.

(Continued)

Table 4.8	DANGERS INHERENT IN PEOPLE-PLEASING BELIEFS (CONT.)

- Because you avoid confrontations at all costs, you are encouraging those around you to repeat the same behaviors that hurt you. If you don't give them the feedback about how you feel, they will never know. They cannot read your mind.

- Because you hold onto a rigid set of beliefs about how people should behave toward you, you invite a life of frustration, disappointment, anger, and resentment.

- Because most of the people with whom you come in contact are not like you, you feel confused, frustrated, and discouraged by their behavior.

- You constantly have to live a double standard, where you treat others with total reverence and respect and somehow rationalize why they don't treat you the same way.

- Because you rationalize that these nonassertive traits are appropriate to teach your children, you are devastated when they say no to you or show angry emotions. You may be quick to blame yourself or your spouse as parental failures because your children are not people pleasers like you.

Note: For more information about these dangers, see *The Disease to Please (Braiker, 1995)*.

R̶x̶ №̶ 32

To help you recognize your assertiveness choices, use the form in Table 4.9 and describe each situation where you had a choice but behaved nonassertively.

♦ ♦ ♦

If you find yourself lacking in assertiveness, there are many steps you can take, starting right now, to modify these behaviors and habits. In Table 4.9, use the A-B-C model once again. Describe the situation in as much detail as possible (A), including what you were feeling emotionally, what you were saying to yourself about the situation (B), and what the consequences of your nonassertive behaviors were (C). Next, be sure to record the eventual outcome of behaving nonassertively (E).

As you become attuned to situations in your life that call for assertive responses where you reacted in a nonassertive manner, you will become sensitive to those situations in the future.

So what else can you do to modify your behaviors to become more assertive? Read a good self-help guide, such as those by Braiker (1995) or Fensterheim and Baer (1975). Braiker's book includes a 21-day action plan for overcoming people-pleasing habits. In their classic book, Fensterheim and Baer give a whole host of ideas for standing up for your right to take care of yourself (asserting yourself) and not feeling as if you must succumb to every request that is made of you. Many times, people pleasers are all-or-nothing thinkers, and they would prefer succumbing to saying "no," which they actually view as an aggressive response.

Table 4.9 — MY NONASSERTIVE RESPONSE RECORD

Examples of how to fill in this table whenever you behave in a nonassertive fashion.

The Day, the Situation, and My Emotions (A)	My Self-Talk (B)	How I Handled the Situation (C)	The Eventual Outcome (E)
Friday 1. I've had plans to go to the lake this weekend with a good friend and we've both been looking forward to it. My manager approached me just before I left the office today and said she could really use my help setting up her garage sale over the weekend. I felt tense all over when she asked for my help.	1. *I'll be letting my manager down if I tell her I can't help her this weekend.* *She may get irritated with me and it could affect our relationship in the office.* *I hope my friend doesn't get angry with me for changing our plans.*	1. I called my friend and explained that I just couldn't turn down my manager, and we could go to the lake the next weekend.	1. My friend said that once I commit to a plan, I should stick to it. She said she couldn't go next weekend. I felt really awful, but what else could I do?

| Table 4.9 | My Nonassertive Response Record (Blank) |

Make copies of this table before you fill it in so you will have tables to fill in every time you behave in a nonassertive fashion.

The Day, the Situation, and My Emotions (A)	My Self-Talk (B)	How I Handled the Situation (C)	The Eventual Outcome (E)
1.			
2.			
3.			

On the contrary, saying no is actually an assertive response, not an aggressive one. An aggressive decline is filled with harshness, sarcasm, and vitriol and often offends the other person. So when your gut tells you that you really don't want to do what someone is requesting of you, do the following:

- **Delay giving an answer.**

    Give yourself at least a day to think about the situation, rather than quickly responding "yes" and then feeling the pressure to do something you really don't want to do. Say you need some time to consider this. This time gives you a feeling of being in control and a chance to rehearse your response. For example, you could say: "I understand your concerns and what you're asking, but I would like some time to think about it and gather more information before I give you an answer."

- **Separate people who are asking from the task they are requesting.**

    Realize that by saying no you are rejecting the task, not the person making the request of you. So if your manager is asking you to volunteer for an additional duty to mentor a young advisor, and you feel overwhelmed with what you have to do already, you can say: "I really appreciate your trusting me with that responsibility, but I can't take on any more tasks right now." You don't need to explain any further, and you do not need to apologize for refusing the request.

- **Decide whether the request or invitation is really in your best interest.**

    What is your true feeling about this request? Being honest with yourself, do you really want to do this?

- **Think about the most likely consequences of saying "yes."**

    This is an important decision point. Would saying "yes" to this request cause any problem for you? If it would, you should politely decline, given the expected consequences of doing so. After deliberating the consequences, if you decide to say "yes" to the request, realize that you made an assertive decision because you stopped and considered all of the likely consequences first.

- **Express your thoughts, opinions, beliefs, and interpretations.**

    State your thoughts and feelings with "I" statements. These statements are assertive expressions of your feelings and decisions, whereas "you" statements are confrontational and accusatory. For example, if your colleague or partner is constantly leaving late for a meeting or engagement, say: "I really get upset when I'm late, and it's important for me to be on time," instead of, "You're always making me late."

$ **State what you want without using words like "always" and "never."**

These words are exaggerations and often make people react to you defensively.

$ **Often you understand the requester's position and need while also wanting to take care of your own needs, so try to find a workable compromise.**

Compromises can involve doing it their way this time and yours the next, or you'll do this if they'll do something for you in return, or you'll do part of what they want and part of what you want.

$ **Continue to use your favorite relaxation technique.**

When you are asserting yourself, it's quite helpful to remain relaxed and in control of your emotions, so keep practicing relaxation techniques.

 ℞ № 33

Take notice and keep a record of situations in which you were assertive, and reward yourself accordingly.

Now let's focus on those times in which you were in a situation that invited an assertive response and you actually chose to do so. Use Table 4.10 on page 96 to record these instances, your self-talk, how you handled the situations, and the eventual outcomes.

Here are some examples of low-anxiety producing ways to begin asserting yourself:

$ **Go into a fast-food establishment (e.g., Burger King) and order only a cup of water.**

Do not order any food. Trust me, they will gladly hand you a cup and direct you to the water, without any hard feelings.

- **Go into a store and ask for change for a dollar.**

    Do not purchase anything. Again, this is your perfect right, and there is no need for you to feel guilty or think you are being unfair to the clerk.

- **Ask a stranger for the time.**

    The best place to do this is in a store or mall. Don't ask, "Do you have the time?" It's better to assert yourself with, "I would appreciate it if you would tell me the time . . . thanks."

- **Force yourself to engage in small talk with someone you don't know very well.**

    Perhaps after a staff meeting or at a social gathering you can practice this by approaching someone you'd like to know better and introducing yourself.

- **When people compliment you or your clothing, politely say, "Thank you."**

    Don't defuse the compliment with a negative or disparaging remark about yourself or your clothing.

- **Compliment people at work.**

    Giving compliments is a great way to begin asserting yourself. This is really a no-lose scenario because everyone loves to receive genuine compliments, and they will like you for doing so.

- **Look people in the eye when you speak to them.**

    If that is difficult for you, imagine a cross on their forehead and look at the cross. People will perceive that you're looking right into their eyes, and as you get more comfortable with this, you can eventually lower your focus right into their eyes.

- **Reward yourself with positive self-talk.**

    After accomplishing each assertive act, talk to yourself with positive and complimentary comments, such as: "I'm really proud of myself" and "This feels great!"

Table 4.10 — My Assertive Response Record

Example of how to use this table. Add your own examples in boxes 2, 3 & 4.

The Day, the Situation, and My Emotions (A)	My Self-Talk (B)	How I Handled the Situation (C)	Ultimate Outcomes (E)
Sunday 1. Mother calls and tells me that her friend's daughters come to visit her much more frequently than I visit her. I feel really angry and guilty at the same time.	1. *My mother is disappointed in me. Maybe she's right, and I'm a lousy daughter.*	1. I told my mother that I understand she's lonely. I love her very much and will spend as much time with her as I can. I would like her to respect me and my needs and not judge me harshly when I don't spend as much time with her as she would like me to.	1. My mother seemed surprised to hear me say that. It actually felt good to stand up for myself. She was upset at first, but then seemed to be calm and asked when I thought I could see her. I felt wonderful being able to share my emotions with her without fear.
2.			
3.			
4.			

Table 4.10 — MY ASSERTIVE RESPONSE RECORD (BLANK)

Make copies of this table before you fill it in so you will have tables to fill in every time you behave in an assertive fashion.

The Day, the Situation, and My Emotions (A)	My Self-Talk (B)	How I Handled the Situation (C)	Ultimate Outcomes (E)
1.			
2.			
3.			
4.			

Treat yourself to something special once you have accumulated five assertive acts, such as buying something you really want but have disciplined yourself to wait for until you "earned" it.

Let's get back to Melanie and Tom, the two advisors with Type-A and people-pleasing personalities, respectively.

Melanie took the advice of a friend and reluctantly agreed to engage in therapy with a professional psychologist. He suggested that she enroll in an evening anger-management course at a local community college. This was an eye-opening experience for her, and she actually used her obsession for being in control and to be perfectly prepared to thrive in each evening's class. The course lasted three months, and at the conclusion of it, her colleagues were amazed at the transformation she'd made, both by observing her in firm meetings and overhearing her speak on the phone with her clients.

Melanie was taught a relaxation technique by her therapist and started taking frequent breaks during each day. She gave herself permission to use her weekends to relax, rather than doing more research in finance and the markets to prepare for the next week. Finally, Melanie worked with her therapist on her need to be perfect. She recognized that letting go of that impossible goal freed her life tremendously, and she realized that she owed it to her body and mind to recharge over the weekends. Despite taking weekends off, her book of business and her career actually blossomed!

As for Tom, he eventually confided in his best friend (another advisor) about how unhappy he was. He admitted that he frequently allowed himself to be manipulated by his clients into doing things that made him uncomfortable, but he was afraid to disagree with them, thinking they would no longer like him and might even fire him. His colleague was stunned because Tom always had a smile on his face and a warm demeanor with everyone in the office.

This friend convinced Tom to get professional help. Ultimately, Tom's psychologist diagnosed him with a "disease-to-please" personality pattern (Braiker, 1995) and showed him how keeping his feelings in and presenting a façade was causing internal disruption in his body. Tom's therapist also conducted assertiveness training with him, and assigned him a classic self-help book, *Don't Say Yes When You Want to Say No* (Fensterheim & Baer, 1975).

Tom began saying "no" when he didn't want to do something, and he stood up for himself when his professional opinion was challenged by a client. He even began to become more assertive with his wife and teenaged children. His stress level in general reduced dramatically, his stomach issues cleared up, and he enjoyed his job like never before. And guess what? He is still adored (and now highly respected) by his clients, colleagues, wife, and children.

ACTION PLAN FOR STRESS MASTERY

Table 4.11   MY ACTION PLAN FOR STRESS MASTERY

Check each one when you've accomplished it. Feel free to add additional new behaviors in the spaces provided.

New Behavior	What I Did and the Date Accomplished
☐ I will use the Type-A behavior checklist to determine whether I exhibit any of these behaviors and if so, I will use the steps discussed in this chapter to modify those behaviors that are detrimental to my stress level. ☐ ☐ ☐	What I did: Date accomplished:
☐ I will use the people-pleasing checklist to determine whether I have exhibited any of these behaviors and if so, I will use the steps discussed in this chapter to modify those behaviors that are detrimental to my stress level. ☐ ☐ ☐	What I did: Date accomplished:

(Continued)

| Table 4.11 | MY ACTION PLAN FOR STRESS MASTERY (CONT.) |

New Behavior	What I Did and the Date Accomplished
☐ I will explore the stress triggers in my life (both in and out of the office), and I will determine the level of tension caused by each. ☐ ☐ ☐	What I did: Date accomplished:
☐ I will use my tables to examine the triggers to my stress and anger and practice disputing the self-talk that leads to my stress and anger. ☐ ☐ ☐	What I did: Date accomplished:
☐ I will use my tables to record my nonassertive responses and practice using assertive responses. ☐ ☐ ☐	What I did: Date accomplished:
☐ I will use my tables to record my assertive responses, and I will reward myself for each five assertive responses I make. ☐ ☐ ☐	What I did: Date accomplished:

How *to* Deflect Stressors: Carefully planned *plus* Warp-Speed Techniques

Wherever you intervene in the stress syndrome, you are acting to break the negative feedback loop. Negative thoughts and physical arousal can no longer escalate into painful emotions. And you have taken a major step toward changing your emotional life.

—Dr. Matthew McKay and Dr. Martha Davis (1981)

LEARNING OBJECTIVES

- I will catch myself "awfulizing" and stop it immediately.

- I will continue to recognize the specific negative-thinking patterns I tend to use when I feel disturbing emotions.

- I will practice organizing my thoughts, looking for patterns, and developing rebuttals using the Thinking-Pattern Worksheet (TPW).

- I will use the thought-stopping, calming-breathing, writing-it-down, or worry-time technique every time I catch myself with negative, self-defeating thoughts.

Deborah embarked on her new trading career with a major brokerage firm after majoring in finance in college. Her parents' advisor counseled her several times over the years about how much money she could make as a broker, and Deborah was excited to get started. The only problem was that during the years that her family's planner was encouraging her, the market was skyrocketing. She wasn't warned about the consequences of inevitable market crashes, nor did the advisor ever warn her about the difficulties she may encounter by entering a predominately male profession.

Since joining the brokerage firm, where there was only one other female broker, the market and the economy became extremely volatile. Deborah realized that making a lot of money was much more challenging than she anticipated. She had recently married and the couple depended on both incomes to make ends meet. She felt like an impostor as she walked into the office full of anxiety each morning.

The pressure to build her book of business as quickly as possible caused much stress for Deborah. She began to have difficulties sleeping and was exhausted at work. Besides her self-imposed depression and anxiety, she was feeling overwhelmed. Was Deborah resilient, or did she succumb and look for a different career? Stay tuned for the rest of the story at the end of the chapter.

Job-related and life stressors are all invitations to feel the emotional and physical symptoms of stress. However, as we discovered in Chapter 3, once you recognize the *habitual patterns* of your automatic thinking in your response to those stressors, you have completed the first step in being able to quickly modify those thoughts and eventually avoid thinking that way in the first place. Remember, the stressors and provocations of life are inevitable; how you react to them is a choice over which you have control.

Learning to modify distorted thoughts and quickly replace them with rational, healthy ones forms the foundation for one of the most revolutionary discoveries in the field of mental health and psychotherapy to appear in the past 50 years: Cognitive Behavioral Therapy and the art of Cognitive Stress Intervention.

Earlier, you learned that the stress an individual feels at any time is only about 10 percent related to recent events in that person's life; but a hefty 90 percent of that stress is related to one's *internal reaction* to those events. Therefore, the key to both reducing stress once it is felt and preventing further stress lies in your internal self-talk—your interpretation of each event, as you perceive it, through the filter of your specific belief system. Cognitive Behavioral Therapy and Cognitive Stress Intervention are cutting-edge strategies directed at quickly reducing and even preventing stress. In this chapter, you will learn five of these powerful strategies.

RECOGNIZE YOUR THINKING PATTERNS

Adopting the right attitude can convert a negative stress into a positive one.

—Hans Seyle (1976)

As you have already learned, automatic, negative-thinking patterns (e.g., catastrophizing, mind reading, blaming) fuel our internal critic, and it has a field day inviting us to be frightened, stressed, angry, depressed, and so on. Some of the specific characteristics that all automatic thinking patterns have in common are as follows:

- $ They are rarely shared with other people. We talk to ourselves differently than we talk to other people. When we talk to ourselves, we tend to use over-generalizations, such as, *No one will ever love me* or *I am a complete failure*.

- $ We usually accept these thoughts unquestionably, believing them even though they are irrational. We don't challenge them unless we have been trained to do so (as in this book), and we act as if they *must* be true if those thoughts went through our minds in the first place. Because we don't challenge these thoughts, they are rarely subjected to logical scrutiny.

- $ They are all learned patterns, and as noted in Chapter 3, we have been told negative things thousands of times while growing up. Often, these thinking patterns are hardwired into us at birth. The patterns then get reinforced and habituated as we hear them from others and repeat them to ourselves.

- $ They tend to be catastrophic. Automatic thoughts tend to lead to other thoughts, triggering a chain of depressive, frightening, overwhelming, and stressful beliefs, emotions, and behaviors, which can be very difficult to overcome. These thoughts tend to *awfulize* a situation, which often underlies our experience of anxiety.

Catch yourself whenever you are "awfulizing" and stop it immediately, using the TPW (Table 5.1) on page 106.

The experience of a negative, painful emotion such as nervousness, anger, depression, fear, unhappiness, or sadness is the first clue that you are engaging in distorted, self-defeating self-talk.

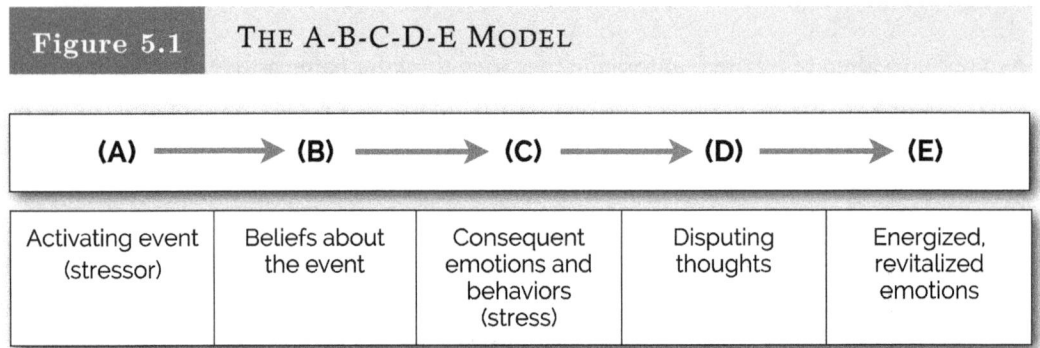

Figure 5.1 THE A-B-C-D-E MODEL

To review (see Figure 5.1), once you experience negative emotions (C), consider those emotions to be a red flag that something happened (A) about which you are talking to yourself negatively (B), and those thoughts need to be examined right now so that you can eventually learn to dispute or rebut them (D). But exactly how do you examine those thoughts and what do you do about them?

Good News!

Using the TPW, you can quickly develop healthy thinking habits, replacing the ones that have been destructive to you.

THE THINKING-PATTERN WORKSHEET (TPW)

"You lick whatever you're up against in life ... not from without in—but from within out!"

—CLAUDE BRISTOL AND HAROLD SHERMAN (AUTHORS)

Using Table 5.1, let's recall Tom from the last chapter, where he comes home mentally exhausted at the end of a day after dealing with several high-value, complaining clients (A). Tom feels overwhelmed, frightened, and worried (C). As you learned earlier, if these emotions are left unchecked, they can lead to a host of physical symptoms, lending to absenteeism—which can become habitual because staying away from the office obviously avoids the stressors and reduces the physical symptoms that originally came about when he felt stressed.

So if Tom does not examine his self-talk (B) about his work situation (A), he could very well begin to get ill and avoid the office—symptoms of burnout.

On the other hand, if Tom does examine his self-talk, he can determine which thoughts are irrational, distorted, and self-defeating. Using the TPW, as soon as Tom recognizes that he is experiencing negative emotions, he writes down those emotions and records the strength of each on a 1–10 scale. Second, he records the automatic thoughts that immediately preceded the emotions, and using the list of 10 thinking-pattern distortions at the bottom of the table, he determines what, if any, distorted-thinking patterns were involved. Notice that I said *if any*. This is because we sometimes have negative, automatic thoughts that are realistic and not distorted.

For example, if a client threatened to move her account away from Tom, it would *not* be a distortion for Tom to think, *There's a good probability that this client will leave my practice and my manager won't be happy about it.* This is the most probable thing that will happen, and it is therefore not a distortion. But the vast majority of our negative thinking is distorted and not based on rational conclusions we have determined. (You can keep handy a copy of Table 3.3 on page 49 to help you remember the definitions of the distorted-thinking patterns.)

As you can see from Tom's TPW—after writing down the situation, his emotions, and the automatic thoughts he can identify—Tom examines them carefully to see if they represent any distorted-thinking patterns. Notice that his first thought is an example of both blowing things out of proportion and intensifying his feelings and arousal. Therefore, these thoughts fall into the patterns of *overgeneralization* and *magnification*.

His second thought is an example of predicting a negative outcome in the future, without really giving himself a chance to explore the probabilities and alternative possibilities (*fortune-telling* or *catastrophizing*).

As Tom predicts what his mentor is likely to do, he is engaging in *fortune-telling*; and then assuming the mentor will no longer work with him, Tom is engaging in the *mind reading* distortion. Finally, fearing that he will fail in his career is another example of the catastrophic thinking pattern of *fortune-telling*.

Once Tom recognizes the distorted, self-defeating thinking patterns that led to the emotions in the first place, it's time to use his creative-thinking skills to come up with rational rebuttals to each of the distorted thoughts (D).

R℞ № 35

The next time you feel any negative emotion (e.g., overwhelm, fright, depression, irritation, impatience, hopelessness), do the following: Use the TPW and describe the event that led to the emotions; write down the specific emotions you feel and rate them. Write down the automatic thoughts that preceded your feeling those emotions, and determine which distortion patterns those thoughts fit. Then write down rebuttal thoughts that make sense. Believing those rebuttal thoughts should help you feel better.

Table 5.1   Tom's Thinking-Pattern Worksheet (TPW)

Description of the activating event (or provocation) (A) that led to his emotional reaction (C):

Tom came home completely drained from the office today. He had to deal with many high-value, complaining clients.

Tom's negative emotions (C) prior to disputing his thoughts and their intensity (1–10):

1. *I'm feeling overwhelmed.* (10)
2. *I'm feeling frightened.* (6)
3. *I'm very worried.* (8)

Automatic Thoughts and Beliefs (B)	Self-Defeating Thinking Pattern	Disputing Responses (Rebuttal) (D)
1. *I had a terrible day at the office today. My prospecting failed to produce a lead, and two clients informed my assistant they were moving on. This is a disaster!*	**a. Overgeneralization** **b. Magnification**	a. *There is no need to magnify or blow this out of proportion. Let's not make it worse than it is. First, it doesn't have to be like this every day. There are many days when I'm quite pleased with my prospecting and I get great feedback from my clients. In addition, I can cope with this and it's not really a disaster. It may be unfortunate, but that's a lot different than a disaster, and I can rebound from this.*

Automatic Thoughts and Beliefs (B)	Self-Defeating Thinking Pattern	Disputing Responses (Rebuttal) (D)
2. I don't think I'm really cut out for this career. I'll never be a successful advisor.	**a. Fortune-telling**	a. Does this experience really mean that I'll never be successful? What are the realistic odds of my not being successful? Are they 90 percent? Are they 10 percent? Where is the evidence to support my fear of failure?
3. I don't know what to do. When my mentor hears about the mistake I made today, he'll probably lose faith in me and want to stop working with me.	**a. Mind reading**	a. This company hired me because the management saw something in me that they predicted would make me successful, and success is not based on doing everything perfectly, every day. I don't have evidence that this incident will make my mentor want to quit.
4. If my mentor quits working with me, I'll fail at this career.	**a. Fortune-telling**	a. If my mentor does decide not to work with me any longer, I can certainly manage on my own now. I have learned much from him and can do the job even without a mentor. If I want one, I can find another.

Negative emotions after rebutting my thoughts and their intensity (1–10):

1. *I'm feeling overwhelmed.* (3)
2. *I'm feeling frightened.* (1)
3. *I'm very worried.* (2)
4. _____
5. _____

Self-Defeating Thinking Patterns: *all or nothing; magnification; mind reading; catastrophizing; being right; should, have to, must; control fallacy; overgeneralization; blaming; emotional reasoning*

Adapted from Matthew McKay and Martha Davis. *Thoughts and Feelings.* 1981, with permission from New Harbinger Press.

In Table 5.1, you see examples of the rebuttal thoughts that Tom came up with. So once he realized that his automatic-thinking patterns in the first column are examples of *overgeneralization* and *magnification*, he considered alternative thoughts that are not self-defeating. For example, instead of telling himself that his work experience that day is a disaster, Tom can see that this is an example of magnification. He can think of different ways of handling the typical stressors that present themselves, and he certainly does not need to interpret what's happening as a *disaster.*

With his second thought, Tom recognizes that he is magnifying his fears of failure way out of proportion. He asks himself the logical question of *Where is the evidence that these unfortunate experiences mean I'll never succeed?* Perhaps he can even brainstorm solutions to his problems with his colleagues, all of whom are experiencing the same stressors.

Tom's rebuttal thoughts include having no evidence that his mentor will quit working with him, and that even if that was the case, he has learned how to be successful in this career—he has many good days and can certainly carry on. He can also find another mentor if he chooses to. These thoughts are very logical and appropriate. Obviously, this rebuttal shows that believing if his mentor quits working with him he will fail in his career is an irrational, catastrophic assumption, which also needs to be eliminated from his thinking. Once all of these negative thoughts are rebutted, he re-examines his emotions and rates their strength again. Usually, the strength is significantly weakened.

When you are doing this for yourself—if you are honest and write rebuttals that you *really believe in*—those emotions either will disappear altogether or will be dramatically reduced in their intensity.

This TPW technique is awkward at first because you are not used to writing down your thoughts, but if you will take the time to write your automatic thoughts whenever you are feeling a negative emotion, then simply look through the list of distorted-thinking patterns at the bottom of the table to see if your thoughts fit one of those categories, you will likely find that there is at least one distortion you are using in your thinking. You can then use all of your creative energies to come up with rebuttals that logically dispute the original thoughts, and these rebuttals are based on logic and evidence. You will then find that your negative feelings will dissolve, as you recognize that your new thoughts make more sense than the original ones. This is the best way to overcome the *internal critic* and keep it from controlling you.

Are you ready to try this method for yourself? First, keep an original and make copies of the TPW in Table 5.2 on the next two pages so you have them for any future situations that may arise.

To practice, use one of the copies and think of a recent situation (A) where you felt a strong, negative emotion, such as anger, frustration, sadness, anxiety, or panic. Write down the situation, the specific emotions you felt (C), and the strength of each emotion from 1 to 10. Next, list as many automatic thoughts and beliefs you can recall that went through your mind before you noticed those emotions (B). Now, look back at the list of negative-thinking patterns from the bottom of the TPW, or from Table 3.3 (pg. 49), and see which ones fit your particular thoughts. Some of your thoughts may not be distortions, but if you think about them objectively, you will see that most are indeed examples of distorted thinking. Finally, write down disputing (rebuttal) thoughts (D), using the examples given in Table 5.1. Think carefully here because coming up with rational rebuttal statements will always help you to defuse your negative emotions about a situation. Finally, re-examine your original emotions and rate their intensity once again. Notice the difference?

If you use the TPW whenever you are feeling strong, negative emotions, it will pay handsome dividends in terms of changing your mood and stress level. Keep practicing this exercise and you will soon learn how to automatically deflect the stress that comes from these unchecked thoughts. You will graduate from using the form to giving yourself instant rebuttal thoughts in your head at warp-speed!

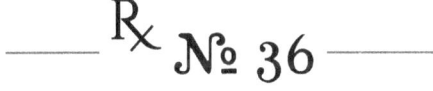 

When you don't have time to use the TPW, use the thought-stopping, calming-breathing, write-it-down, or worry-time techniques described next.

| Table 5.2 | MY THINKING-PATTERN WORKSHEET (TPW) |

Make copies of this table before you fill it in so you can use it every time you feel stressed.

Description of the situation that led to my emotional reaction (A):

Negative emotions (C) prior to rebutting my thoughts and their intensity (1–10):
1. _____

2. _____

3. _____

Table 5.2	MY THINKING-PATTERN WORKSHEET (TPW) (CONT.)	

Automatic Thoughts and Beliefs (B)	Self-Defeating Thinking Pattern	Disputing Responses (Rebuttal) (D)
1.	a. b.	1.
2.	a. b.	2.
3.	a. b.	3.
4.	a. b.	4.

If you have more than four thoughts, continue the section above on another sheet.

Negative emotions (C) after rebutting my thoughts and their intensity 1–10:

1. _____
2. _____
3. _____
4. _____
5. _____

Self-Defeating Thinking Patterns: *all or nothing; magnification; mind reading; catastrophizing; being right; should, have to, must; control fallacy; overgeneralization; blaming; emotional reasoning*

Adapted from Matthew McKay and Martha Davis. *Thoughts and Feelings.* 1981, with permission from New Harbinger Press.

A THOUGHT-STOPPING TECHNIQUE

Thoughts repeated become believed. Thoughts believed become reality.

—UNKNOWN

Obviously, there are many times when you are working, driving, or in a store and you cannot easily write down the negative thoughts you realize are occurring at that moment. In situations like that, you can employ a rapid method for stopping these thoughts in their tracks, without the necessity of using a TPW to analyze the cause of your emotional reactions.

Here is a technique I have used with clients for more than 30 years, and it really works (Mahoney, 1971). Get a thick, number 64 rubber band—the kind used to wrap bundles of mail. Write a positive thought on the rubber band such as, "Just relax, this will pass," and associate this positive thought with the rubber band. Wear the rubber band on your wrist.

The second purpose of the rubber band is the most important. Whenever you recognize thoughts that are distorted and get you upset, pull back on the band, snap it on your wrist, and at the same time, shout in your head: *Stop this silly thinking!* Once the thought stops, immediately take a couple of deep breaths in through your nose and out through your mouth, relaxing your body while telling yourself a disputing positive thought.

As an example, let's say you're in the middle of your workday and you are feeling angry and irritable. When you have time for a break, you stop and focus on what you were just thinking. *My manager doesn't really give two cents about me and my clients who are defiant and hostile toward me when the market tanks. I'm on my own here.* This is the time to snap the rubber band, take a series of deep breaths, and as you exhale and calm down, tell yourself something like this: *I don't have any evidence that my manager doesn't give two cents about me. She has to spread her attention around to many advisors and each has important issues. Eventually, she'll get around to me. I just need to stay on her radar screen.*

A CALMING-BREATHING TECHNIQUE

As you recall from Chapter 1, when we feel provoked, we switch on the sympathetic nervous system (SNS), which includes rapid breathing. The important thing to remember is that rapid breathing is necessary for dealing with real emergencies because we need to rapidly transmit oxygen to our brains to make quick decisions. But when we switch on the SNS because of our negative internal dialogue, there is no real emergency and, therefore, no need for rapid breathing. In fact, such rapid breathing is usually shallow breathing (only the chest and shoulders move), which can increase the tension and discomfort you feel. So one of the best things we can do whenever we feel strain and upsetting emotions is to practice a *calming-breathing* technique, where you get a full volume of air, beginning in your abdomen and moving up. Here it is:

Fold your hands over your stomach area and take a slow, deep breath in through your nose, hold it for four seconds, and then exhale through your mouth for seven seconds. Are your hands moving out as you breathe in and moving back in as you exhale? If not, practice over and over, as if you are filling a glass from the bottom up. Close your eyes and imagine there is a balloon inside your abdomen. Each time you inhale, imagine the balloon filling with air.

Whenever you are sitting or reclining, practice this type of breathing by folding your hands over your stomach. Once you find your hands moving as you inhale and exhale, you've mastered it! Practice every day until this becomes part of your natural breathing style.

WRITE-IT-DOWN TECHNIQUE

Set a time, several times a week, when you will write down your feelings and thoughts. Putting your feelings into words you can read helps you sort out the rational from irrational ones. It also gives you a sense of release.

Make a specific schedule for your writing time. For example, you may want to spend 10 or 15 minutes writing down your feelings and thoughts about your day just before retiring for the evening. Be sure that your writing place is one where you won't be interrupted or disturbed. Perhaps reserve a private file on your computer for this daily exercise. You don't need to share the writings with anyone, so you can feel free to explore your deepest thoughts and feelings.

Write freely what comes into your mind, without worrying about grammar, spelling, or the like. This can be a truly cathartic experience for you. If writing seems too much of a chore, record your thoughts and feelings into a recorder. Simply saying them aloud will help calm you.

WORRY-TIME TECHNIQUE

Many people worry throughout the day, constantly setting off their SNS, resulting in mood and stress fluctuations that fill their days. Here is a simple technique that works well to prevent this: Choose a *worry time* of a maximum of 10 minutes each day. Save up all of your worries and think about them only during this 10-minute time period. Try to use a "safe time," such as just when you get home from the office, rather than right before going to bed. Realize that constant worrying accomplishes nothing positive, so cramming it all into this 10-minute worry time will free yourself for the rest of your waking day. The key to this method is to force yourself to only worry during this worry time. If worries enter your mind after your worry time, stop them in their tracks and tell yourself that you will save them for the next day's worry time.

MAKE A CONTRACT WITH YOURSELF

Reward yourself for successfully warding off worry and stress using the techniques listed in this chapter. Do a pleasant activity as a reward (e.g., go to a bookstore or coffee shop). You can even make morning activities that you must do (e.g., brush your teeth, comb your hair) contingent on completion of one or two of the Stress Mastery Prescriptions listed in this chapter and throughout the book. Write out the contract for yourself on your computer and keep it on your screen.

When you stick to such a contract, there is a great incentive to practice your new stress-mastery skills because you *have* to brush your teeth and comb your hair before you leave for the office in the morning. Always do the thing you are procrastinating *first*. Don't fool yourself into thinking, *I'll do it right after I comb my hair.*

So what happened to Deborah? Recall that she was feeling overwhelmed in her broker's role because of the economy and pressure to earn more money without consistent results, plus she was feeling out of place as a woman in a man's world. In some ways, she felt like an impostor (Clance, 1985) in her male-dominated firm. She had plenty of physical and emotional reasons to quit her job and seek a new career.

Fortunately, Deborah viewed this awful start to her career as a challenge. She thought long and hard about how she could get clients to trust her, and she sought advice from another female in the firm.

Deborah also consulted with me about her fears of failure, depression, and anxiety. I taught her many of the same techniques you have already read about in this chapter, including taking change of her self-talk by using the Thinking-Pattern Worksheet, calming technique, thought stopping, and making a contract with herself.

In a few weeks, Deborah was no longer overwhelmed by things over which she had no control, such as unpredictable market fluctuations. With the help of her female colleague, Deborah armed herself with expertise in products for retirement, marketed her services mainly to people approaching retirement, and began to build a nice book of business. This, of course, raised her self-confidence. She no longer felt like an impostor in a man's world.

Instead of feeling overwhelmed and hopeless, Deborah began to feel in control of both her career and her emotions. And when she had those dreary days, she would come home and write down her feelings and thoughts. She also made it a habit to remember those special moments when she received letters or personal visits from past clients who told her how she had a profound impact on their lives and their families' security. She felt valued and appreciated.

ACTION PLAN FOR STRESS MASTERY

Table 5.3 My Action Plan for Stress Mastery

Check each one when you've accomplished it. Feel free to add additional new behaviors in the spaces provided.

New Behavior	What I Did and the Date Accomplished
☐ I will catch myself "awfulizing" and stop it immediately. ☐ ☐ ☐	What I did: Date accomplished:
☐ Every day I will continue to recognize the specific negative-thinking patterns I tend to use when I feel disturbing emotions. ☐ ☐ ☐	What I did: Date accomplished:

☐	I will practice organizing my thoughts, looking for patterns, and developing rebuttals using the Thinking-Pattern Worksheet (TPW).	What I did:
☐		
☐		
☐		Date accomplished:
☐	I will use the thought-stopping, calming-breathing, writing-it-down, make-a-contract, and worry-time techniques every time I catch myself with negative moods or emotions.	What I did:
☐		
☐		
☐		Date accomplished:

PART II

PRESCRIPTIONS *for* BUILDING YOUR PSYCHOLOGICAL IMMUNITY *to* STRESS

6

How to Harness the Power Within and Inoculate Yourself Against the Impact of Inevitable Stressors

What lies behind us and what lies before us are tiny matters compared to what lies within us.

—Oliver Wendell Holmes, author and poet

LEARNING OBJECTIVES

- I will become aware of the thinking patterns that provoke stress within me.
- I will learn the three Cs of stress hardiness and tips for building commitment, control, and challenge.
- I will learn how to use the components of self-efficacy to buffer myself against stress.

(continued)

> (continued)
> + I will learn how to use the power of goal setting to increase my stress hardiness.
> + I will understand the eight questions to ask myself regarding each goal I set.
> + I will learn how to use the power of positive affirmations to enhance my hardiness.

Danny is a classic example of an individual who has found a way to inoculate himself against the inevitable challenges he faces as a financial advisor. He came into the financial advising arena from retail, where he was forced to "reinvent" his store several times a year. For example, he had to order his winter and Christmas goods in the summertime and prepare for his summer sales in the winter and spring. Such constant changes can be quite challenging. Just as you are adjusting to the trials and tribulations of running a big store, you need to adapt to changing displays and making room for goods that will be on those displays, even though you are months away from the change.

Danny had a brother in the life insurance business who convinced him to give it a whirl. What did Danny bring with him from his retail experience that really helped him adjust to the rigors of a life insurance agent? Was he already "inoculated" against certain stressors because of that experience? Read on ...

HOW TO BEGIN THE INOCULATION PROCESS

What your eyes see and your ears hear, if seen and heard often enough, you remember ...
and make a part of your life.
—Claude Bristol (1987)

Just as being inoculated against diseases builds our resilience and protects us from those diseases, *psychological inoculation* means developing skills to help you resist stressors and build your resistance to their impact. Resilience to stress begins with repetition of *positive* thoughts, beliefs, and images. Doing this will begin to change your attitude and confidence. As I am so fond of saying, your dreams have no barriers, and the only difference between your dreams and your reality is the presence of your internal critic and the resultant lack of confidence.

HOW TO BUILD RESILIENCE TO STRESS: THE THREE C'S OF STRESS HARDINESS

> *In the middle of every difficulty lies an opportunity.*
> —ALBERT EINSTEIN

In Chapter 4, you learned about two types of personalities that are very prone to stress—unless, that is, they become aware of them and focus on changing their habitual responses when they're provoked.

Indeed, there are also some folks who fortunately are hardwired with stress-*resistant* traits. Maddi (2002, 2006) coined the term *stress hardiness* to refer to these people.

But just as those genetically predisposed with stress-prone personalities can learn to modify their behaviors, people can learn to develop stress-resistant traits, even if they weren't born stress hardy. This hardiness is made up of three components: *commitment*, *control*, and *challenge*. Together, these three components empower people to become resilient, despite experiencing the inevitable provocations and stressors of life (Khoshaba & Maddi, 1999; Maddi, 2002).

Good News!

Even if you were not born hardwired with the three Cs (which many astronauts and test pilots are, for example), you can learn to develop these characteristics as adults. The result is that you will thrive, even in the face of highly stressful provocations. This is the difference between the advisor who gets overwhelmed and the one who thrives under virtually the same stress-provoking situations.

1. COMMITMENT

Let's say you decided to become a financial advisor because of a close relative who took you under his wing and encouraged you to join a profession where you would make a wonderful living, while having the long-term goal of genuinely helping clients feel secure regarding their financial futures. This career field offered you vision and purpose in life. Now, ask yourself if your actual work as a financial advisor has relevance to your long-term goals. Most likely, the answer is yes. Individuals who are committed to both short- and long-term goals, and *stay committed* regardless of unfortunate events and the resultant negative thoughts that creep into their minds, are the most successful people. Committed advisors see the real value in staying focused on their goals, even when the stress mounts (Maddi, 2008).

Advisors who possess or develop this trait are committed to their work and stay focused on the value they are providing their clients, regardless of the feedback they may (or may not) receive from those clients.

Commit yourself to a few years at a time, and pour all of your energy into that relatively short commitment. At the end of that time frame, you can decide whether you want to recommit or leave the profession. But by committing to a specific time frame, you won't risk feeling overwhelmed or burned out. You might be surprised at how devoted you will become when there is a reasonable reconsideration time built into your life plan.

Engaging more deeply in working relationships with your colleagues, managers, and mentors will help you feel like an integral part of the firm, as well as make a commitment to your client base.

2. CONTROL

Stress-hardy advisors are *inner*-directed, meaning they believe they are in control of their own destiny. They enjoy being able to make decisions related to their work, as opposed to being micromanaged by supervisors.

Stress-hardy advisors look at stressors as *motivators* so that they can turn the stressors to their advantage and even gain more control. They keep trying to influence outcomes, rather than feeling powerless or at the whim of situations over which they have little control, such as market fluctuations (Maddi, 2008).

Again, a strong working relationship with your colleagues, managers, and mentors can buffer you against job stressors over which you feel little control.

3. CHALLENGE

Stress-hardy people see stress as part of life, and they see such challenges as *opportunities* to learn how to grow, *despite* the stress. They aren't rattled when their comfort is disrupted (Maddi, 2008).

Life is full of obstacles. When I decided to write this book, I gave myself a series of deadlines. My main goal was to get this book out quickly and into the hands of advisors all over the world. The easiest thing to do would have been to look at this task as overwhelming and too difficult to accomplish in a short period of time. I could have begged off the assignment and given myself more time so that I could do the other things

I love to do. However, this would be giving in to my internal critic, forcing me to procrastinate because of fear that I would not be able to accomplish the task on time.

Instead, I forced myself to look at this as a *challenge* and continued to focus on how wonderful I would feel once I had completed the task. Successful people consistently look at obstacles as challenges, as opposed to being overwhelmed by those obstacles. Feeling overwhelmed leads to more negative thinking, ultimately leading to procrastination to avoid the anticipated failure.

Advisors who learn to be stress-hardy view obstacles as challenges, not as insurmountable roadblocks. They thrive on overcoming their challenges, rather than giving up. So, continually reminding yourself about the value you are bringing to your clients and their families (and descendants) adds to your personal vision and purpose in life. If this has been a struggle for you, look for resources to help you overcome those challenges, such as the guidelines described next.

THE POWER OF SELF-EFFICACY

> *A strong sense of efficacy enhances human accomplishment and personal well-being in many ways. People with high assurance in their capabilities approach difficult tasks as challenges to be mastered rather than as threats to be avoided.*
>
> —BANDURA (1994)

There is powerful research by world-renowned psychologist, Robert Bandura, that shows much promise for helping to build stress hardiness. Perceived self-efficacy is your confident belief that you can indeed achieve your goals and dreams and that in doing so, have influence over events that affect your life. So as an advisor, the belief is that whatever challenges you face, even those over which you have little control, you *truly* believe in your ability to rise to the challenge and make good things happen. This leads not only to the development of stress hardiness, but also physical hardiness, as barriers to stress.

This strong, confident belief system includes the belief that you definitely have choices over your responses to events that affect your life. Obviously, what you have learned in Part I of this book will contribute to this belief.

It's worth repeating: People with a strong belief in their capabilities "approach difficult tasks as *challenges* to be mastered, rather than as threats to be avoided" (Bandura, 1994). They remain *committed* to their challenging goals and view setbacks as temporary, quickly recovering from them and heightening their efforts accordingly. Their perception is that the setback resulted from insufficient effort or knowledge on their part, both of which they *can* control. They also believe they can exercise control over most threatening situations they will face. Self-efficacy, then, embraces all three components of psychological hardiness: commitment, control, and challenge.

℞ № 37 — *Don't try to control that which cannot be controlled or things that have already happened. Stick with what you are capable of controlling in the present.*

HOW CAN YOU DEVELOP A RESILIENT SENSE OF SELF-EFFICACY?

Self-efficacy is developed and enriched by three main sources: mastery experiences, modeling influences, and your perception of your emotional state at any time.

1. MAXIMIZE YOUR MASTERY EXPERIENCES AND MINIMIZE YOUR DISAPPOINTMENTS.

This seems obvious, but it is important to remember experiences in which you are extremely successful when you judge yourself (e.g., landing a high-value referral using creative means that you learned from a mentor), and in situations where you are disappointed, learn how you will handle it differently next time and then forget about it. Each time you are successful adds to your self-efficacy beliefs, giving you a psychological Teflon coating for inevitable disappointments.

2. COPY ROLE MODEL AND MENTOR SUCCESS STRATEGIES.

You do not have to reinvent the wheel to be successful. Thriving colleagues in your firm or advisor networking association are flattered when you copy their blueprints. And your manager wants you to be successful, so don't be afraid to model her style either. All of these people started out like you did. They learned how to deal with the inevitable slings and arrows of the advisor business, and so will you.

3. Take Charge of Your Moods and Emotions.

Maintaining a positive mood enhances self-efficacy. Having emotional ups and downs and feeling out of control emotionally makes one feel vulnerable and erodes self-efficacy. When you are about to call a difficult client, the arousal you feel can be interpreted as energizing because you expect a successful interaction (high self-efficacy), rather than as anxiety because you anticipate embarrassment or anger during the call (low self-efficacy).

Which of these athletes do you suppose is more successful prior to his event: the athlete who feels tension and sees it as excited anticipation of a good performance, or the one who feels tension and expects to have difficulty in the event? You know the answer … and the way you think and talk to yourself about an event is always *your* choice!

Re-read Chapter 3 and make sure you continue to follow its Action Plan. Doing so will keep your moods and emotions under control, thus helping you maintain your strong sense of self-efficacy.

Of course, there are direct parallels between self-efficacy beliefs—taking control of your internal critic, eradicating the "Impostor Fear," the three Cs of hardiness, and goal setting, which you will learn about later in this chapter.

Table 6.1 gives examples of positive thoughts that lead to these remarkable outcomes for advisors. I have left spaces for you to fill in additional positive statements about yourself.

Table 6.1   Examples of Self-Efficacy Thoughts

Add your own thoughts in the spaces provided.

1. *When I listen carefully and understand the concerns and goals of each client, I am able to appease even the most difficult ones most of the time.*

1a. _____

1b. _____

(continued)

2. *I am convinced that, with more experience, I will continue to become more and more capable of successfully addressing my clients' needs and goals.*

2a. _____
_____

2b. _____
_____

3. *I know that I can maintain a positive relationship with my clients, even when tensions arise. I reframe catastrophic concerns of my clients into realistic expectations.*

3a. _____
_____

3b. _____
_____

4. *I am proactive and realistic with my clients. I use several media, including quarterly client events, a weekly newsletter, client conference calls, and personal calls to contact my clients before, during, and after market declines.*

4a. _____
_____

4b. _____
_____

Good News!

There are many additional ways to develop a sense of stress hardiness and self-efficacy. Table 6.2 provides some proven ideas.

To develop stress hardiness and self-efficacy, you must believe in yourself and understand that *you* have the ultimate control over your thoughts and beliefs.

Besides the three methods of enhancing your self-efficacy discussed above, here are more behaviors that can help you develop the attitudes of commitment, control, and challenge.

Table 6.2 SIX ADDITIONAL WAYS TO DEVELOP STRESS HARDINESS AND SELF-EFFICACY

1. Study colleagues who seem to be very resilient to the stressors inherent in their advising careers. Try to learn how they cope or manage those stressors. Watching a colleague who is similar to you, in a similar situation yet more successful, will help convince you that you, too, possess the capabilities to master comparable challenges.

2. Make a list of colleagues who are *deficient* in attitudes of stress hardiness, and study how they deal with similar stressors. Obviously, you'll want to make sure you do *not* model their behavior, but rather begin modeling the behavior of the resilient folks with whom you work.

3. Focus on each successful accomplishment you have. Successes build the belief that you can master such problems in the future. Pay attention to the people around you who build you up and tell you that you have what it takes. Continually give yourself positive feedback, and focus on feedback both from others who recognize the wonderful job you're doing and from your clients, who ultimately benefit from what you have done. As far as negative feedback goes, take what you need in order to improve and let it go. Too often we make the mistake of giving much more importance to negative feedback than we do to the positive feedback we receive.

4. When times are tough in your job, stick to your plan. You will emerge much stronger by working through this adversity.

5. Always look for the silver lining in every dark cloud you face in your job.

6. Always look at stress-provoking situations in your job as *opportunities* to use your abilities to solve those problems.

HOW TO USE THE POWER OF GOAL SETTING TO STAY FOCUSED DESPITE STRESS PROVOCATIONS

With goals, you become what you want. Without them, you remain what you were.

—LEE PULOS (2004)

Research cited by Dr. David Burns (1989) shows that you are approximately 11 times more likely to follow through on goals if you write them down and regularly revisit them, as opposed to just thinking about them in your head.

Realistic goal setting helps remove helpless feelings, creates a positive future, breathes life into that future, and helps you to visualize that future. Successful people are willing to transform themselves, change, and grow, and goal setting helps accomplish those ends. For example, elite athletes can recite the series of goals they set for themselves to get to the top of their sport. But we all sometimes unconsciously sabotage ourselves in the quest to accomplish our goals.

 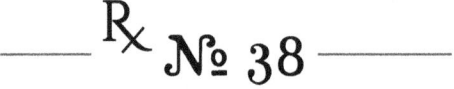

Make a list of your short- and long-term goals, right now, and answer the eight questions listed in Table 6.3 for each goal.

Table 6.3 is a list of eight questions to ask yourself about each goal. These questions will help you define your goal and realize how you have been unconsciously sabotaging yourself in the past. Use a separate sheet of paper (or file on the computer) for each goal you have, and be sure to write your responses to these eight questions for each goal you have.

I am indebted to one of my mentors, Dr. Lee Pulos (2004), for developing many of the ideas contained in this table.

Read your goals aloud to yourself 10 times *each day*. Don't put this off. *Today* is your point of power where you can create the optimal future for yourself. So when you focus on future goals and imagine them becoming a reality soon, you are able to release all of the obstacles that held you back from accomplishing these goals before. In short, release the past (failures to achieve) and imagine each goal taking place *now*.

Table 6.3   QUESTIONS TO ASK YOURSELF REGARDING EACH GOAL

My Questions	My Answers
Write down your goal:	
1. Why do I want to achieve this goal?	1.
2. What are three things that will happen to let me know that I have achieved this goal?	2.
3. What will I hear others say that will let me know I have achieved my goal?	3.
4. What kinds of things will I say to myself once I have achieved my goal?	4.
5. What feelings/emotions will I be experiencing on attainment of my goal?	5.
6. How can I sabotage myself in my quest for this goal?	6.

(continued)

Table 6.3	Questions to Ask Yourself (cont.)
7. *What quality(s) do I need to develop in myself to achieve my goal?*	7.
8. *What small gesture or step can I make to act as if I'm already on my way toward achieving my goal?*	8.

THE POWER OF DESIRE, IMAGINATION, AND EXPECTATION

When you set realistic goals for yourself and you're serious about accomplishing them, you're releasing a "slumbering giant" of potential that has been residing within, waiting to express itself. This represents all of the latent talent and creativity you have kept locked up inside because of your self-doubt and your internal belief that your fate in life was sealed years ago. You can throw off the shackles of self-doubt, fear, and intimidation by sustaining your desire to attain your goals, expecting that you *will* achieve them, and by using your imagination to visualize yourself as you will be once you attain those goals.

So when you write down your goals, keep in mind that you need to have the fire and passion to accomplish them (desire), rather than targeting these goals because someone else in your life has decided that you should work on them. When you lie down to retire each evening, just when you are in that sleepy state between awake and asleep, visualize (an example of imagination) yourself as if you have already accomplished your goals. Feel all of the happy emotions connected with that vision as if this is your reality today, and act as if what you want has already happened. This brings the future into the present.

Finally, anticipate (expectation) that you will succeed. Nothing awakens the slumbering giant as much as expecting success. Releasing these three keys is a continual process that you can practice each day. Try it—you'll be amazed at the results.

People who worry about situations over which they will never have control cannot easily develop the three Cs, and they ultimately lose faith in their ability to achieve their goals. Accordingly, regardless of the lack of positive feedback you receive from others, *each day* you should reflect on your accomplishments and achievements and give yourself a pat on the back. One way to make this happen much easier is by using positive affirmations (Fishel, 2003).

HOW TO USE THE POWER OF POSITIVE AFFIRMATIONS TO DEVELOP THE THREE C'S AND ACCOMPLISH YOUR GOALS

> *Thoughts of your mind have made you what you are, and thoughts of your mind will make you what you become from this day forward.*
>
> —CATHERINE PONDER, AUTHOR

Positive affirmations are specific, positive statements that you make to yourself. The problem is that most people engage in negative self-talk about themselves more than running positive affirmations through their minds.

Affirmations can be written on 3x5 cards, typed on your computer desktop, or (ideally) recorded so you can listen to your voice articulating them over and over.

For maximum effectiveness, Fishel (2003) recommends that each affirmation must be:

- positive
- uttered with gusto, power, and conviction
- said in the here and now (present)
- possible to attain
- only about you, not others

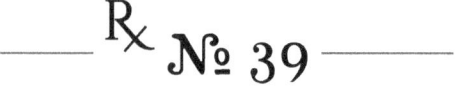

To develop attitudes of hardiness, and to stick to your goals, start using positive affirmations daily. Write down or record your affirmations and read or listen to them at least 10 times a day for a minimum of 21 days.

"Countless experiments have proven that change occurs within 21 days when we repeat our affirmation at least ten times each day" (Fishel, 2003, p. 18). The key to this dramatic finding is repeating the affirmation(s) at least ten times each day, for 21 *consecutive* days.

As you now know, the SNS goes into emergency mode whenever we even *think* about something that concerns us, so our subconscious mind doesn't know the difference between a real threat and one that is imagined through our self-talk. Think about and visualize going to your high school or college reunion and spotting a dear friend you haven't seen in years. Now, close your eyes and try to visualize that moment actually happening. Do you feel an instant chill or warm feeling coming over you?

Now think about cuddling your pet or sitting on a beach with a gentle breeze in your hair, watching a marvelous sunset. How do these thoughts and images make you feel physically? You can see that your thoughts bring about images, and those images rapidly lead to physical changes in your body. As Ruth Fishel (2003) says, "Words can block us from success or bring us success" (p. 10).

In Chapters 3 and 5, you learned how to recognize typical negative-thinking patterns in which you frequently engage and how to stop them. Now, you can go beyond that to develop *positive* thoughts (affirmations), which can become habits—part of your daily life. Think these thoughts when you are getting dressed, on the way to the office, during breaks in your workday, on your way home, and before you retire for the evening.

As with your goals, you can use several reminders for your affirmations: Keep a separate notebook to write them down, type them on the computer, have your computer bring them up on your desktop each day, have sticky notes on the frame of your computer screen to remind you to write them down each day, or record them into a cassette or digital recorder so you can actually hear them in your own voice several times a day.

You can use your creativity and your own specific needs to create your affirmations. Here are some examples by category to give you a jump start:

COMMITMENT

- *I'm committed to reviewing this book weekly to build my resilience to stress.*
- *I'm committed to observing others I admire and modeling their successful behavior.*
- *I'm committed to staying at my job and making a difference in the lives of my clients and their families, despite the obstacles I face.*

CONTROL

- *I'm ultimately in control of my mind and body.*
- *I recognize my "internal critic," and I know how to control it.*
- *I know what I can control and what I cannot. I only focus on what I can control.*

CHALLENGE

- *I look at stress-provoking situations on my job as opportunities to use my untapped abilities to solve them.*
- *I thrive on challenges, as my ability to creatively solve those challenges flows easily and effortlessly.*
- *I embrace obstacles as challenges and challenges as opportunities to succeed.*

GOALS

- *I set realistic and challenging goals, write them down, and review them every day.*
- *My goals are specific. The more specific they are, the easier it is for me to visualize myself accomplishing them.*
- *I'm passionate about my goals, and I expect to accomplish them.*

CHANGE

- *I see every change in my job or responsibilities as a new opportunity to achieve my goals.*
- *I know what I can change and what I cannot. I only focus on what I can change.*
- *I recognize what I would like to change in my life, and I'll focus on that every day.*

CONFIDENCE

- *I'm confident in my ability to overcome obstacles today.*
- *I'm learning to trust my own wisdom, creativity, and intelligence and give myself permission to take realistic risks in my life.*
- *My confidence is growing daily.*

BELIEVING IN MYSELF

- *If I ever had any doubts about myself in the past, today is a great day to cast them aside and throw away any disbelief that has ever held me back.*

- *I know that my success is 100 percent up to me. I'm a winner because I now know how to look at events in my life and what to say to myself about them.*

- *I will stand up for myself, believe in myself, and succeed in whatever I wish. I know I can do it. I am focused and confident.*

So, how did Danny adjust to the rigors of financial advising after coming from a retail store background? As it turned out, he was fortunate because the retail experience, with its inevitable changes and challenges—plus the long hours—did inoculate Danny against many of the same stressors waiting for him in his new advising role. After 34 years in advising, he says that he sees all challenges as opportunities, and is therefore not frightened by those challenges.

The insurance company whose products he primarily recommends for his clients also reinvents itself periodically with new products. Rather than feeling overwhelmed by those changes, he views them as *opportunities* to adapt to a new regime in the company. Therefore, his attitude remains positive, regardless of the challenges.

Over the years, Danny has sought out mentors and asked them for candid feedback from which he could learn. He believes that "success leaves footprints." He still recalls not being prepared for a meeting early in his career and having his mentor give him some direct, difficult to hear constructive feedback. That humbling moment challenged him and as a result he never made that mistake again. He has thanked that mentor many times for that defining moment when he could have quit, but he instead used the feedback as motivation.

Danny sees his business as being one of relationship building and he takes that very seriously. Accordingly, he has remained totally committed to his clients over the years.

ACTION PLAN FOR STRESS MASTERY

Table 6.4 — MY ACTION PLAN FOR STRESS MASTERY

Check each one when you've accomplished it. Feel free to add additional new behaviors in the spaces provided.

New Behavior	What I Did and the Date Accomplished
☐ Every day I will watch for specific stress-provoking thoughts and stop them immediately, using the rubber-band technique. ☐ ☐ ☐	What I did: Date accomplished:
☐ I will use the tips I learned in Table 6.2 to develop my attitudes of commitment, control, and challenge. ☐ ☐ ☐	What I did: Date accomplished:
☐ I will write down or record short- and long-term goals and review them daily. I will affirm each of my goals aloud 10 times a day. ☐ ☐ ☐	What I did: Date accomplished:

(continued)

| Table 6.4 | MY ACTION PLAN FOR STRESS MASTERY (CONT.) |

☐	For each goal I write down, I will ask myself the eight key questions and write down the answers.	What I did:
☐		
☐		
☐		Date accomplished:
☐	I will make a list of positive affirmations, look at them each day, recite them aloud at least 10 times each day, rewrite and/or record them, and listen to them in my own voice each day.	What I did:
☐		
☐		
☐		Date accomplished:

How to Select and Retain Ideal Clients

*Re-examine all you have been told.
Dismiss what insults your soul.*

—Walt Whitman, poet, essayist, and journalist

LEARNING OBJECTIVES

- I will be able to determine which clients cause me the most stress and understand if they possess toxic personality traits.
- I will be able to use tactful, respectful communications in order to eliminate those clients from my practice.
- I will learn several ways to attract female clients to my practice.
- I will learn "active listening" techniques in order to service all of my clients better.
- I will understand the core values that underlie my wealth management/enhancement strategies, and I will maintain those values despite temptations to compromise them.
- If I have clients whose investment goals and needs do not resonate well with my core values, I will refer them to other advisors.

Since so much of your stress comes from dealing with your clients' complaints, ignorance, and emotional investment requests/demands, it makes sense to carefully choose clients who resonate with and are in harmony with your core wealth management/enhancement philosophies. It's also crucial to weed out those who are constant sources of stress for you.

David is a 39-year-old highly successful advisor who has spent his 13 years in the business dealing with the key stressors that go with the territory, such as unpredictable markets and emotionally driven expectations from clients.

In order to get a jump-start on world events, David, based in California, rises at 4 a.m. and is in the office by six. Obsessively driven to respond to every email he receives from clients, he often doesn't leave the office before 7 p.m., and then he comes home hoping to spend a bit of quality time with his wife and children before they all retire for the evening. He admits to sometimes skipping breakfast and lunch and to sleep deprivation, all of which are unfortunate characteristics of David's Type-A personality.

Yet despite all of this, David is extremely successful. In fact, he was a million dollar producer in only his fifth year in the business. This is largely due to his intelligence, his obsessive desire to hone his knowledge each day, the amazing amount of time and commitment he devotes to his clients, and his courage to *cut certain clients loose* from his practice. But how does David keep his stress levels manageable? You'll learn his secrets throughout this chapter.

It took me many years to realize that my unwillingness to turn away any clients who were referred to me exacerbated my own stress level dramatically. Partly because of my desire to make as much income as possible, partly because I didn't want to ever disappoint a referral source, and partly because of my irrational belief that I could help *anyone* who came through my door, I maintained many clients my gut warned me about. When I knew these clients were on my calendar for the day, I could feel the stress building inside. I filled my mind with negative thoughts and fortune-telling messages about how difficult it would be to make it through that tortuous hour. No matter how much I used my own knowledge about my internal critic to control my inner dialogue, as well as my knowledge of psychotherapy, I couldn't modify the behavior or personalities of these clients, so the stress caused by working with them continued.

I had my share of clients who complained about severe anxiety or depression, for example, and they asked me to help them, yet they were simply unwilling to change their own distorted-thinking patterns that led to those emotions, and they wouldn't follow my advice. I also counseled many people with personality styles that made them very difficult to deal with—yet, I persisted.

Many people bounce from psychologist to psychologist, looking for some panacea or quick fix for their issues, without the desire to carefully examine themselves or change any of their self-defeating habits. My experience suggests that working with such clients is an exercise in futility. The fact of the matter is that *behaviors* can be modified, if the individual chooses to diligently work on modifying them, but personalities do not change and are not really modifiable. And when those personalities or traits are *toxic*, these clients can become extremely challenging. It took years, but once I made a commitment to carefully weed out cases I predicted would be problems for me, and began to dismiss clients whose treatment was going nowhere or who possessed toxic personalities, my stress levels decreased dramatically.

We are hardwired with our personalities, such as the *Type-A* and *people-pleasing* personalities I described in Chapter 4. These personality types are not toxic, per se; it is only when people demonstrate behaviors that are actually noxious to your mental (and physical) well-being that I refer to them as *toxic*. Add to this the discord of *your own* personality traits and the possibilities for daily frustration become exacerbated, where succumbing to stress and burnout multiply exponentially. Many advisors are hesitant to send any business away, thus putting up with unbearable, demanding, self-centered clients whose personalities inevitably lead to stressful interactions.

Authors describe "Investor Styles" of clients (e.g., Cass, et al, 2008), and they point to such characteristics as "risk taking vs. risk averse," "micro-managing vs. laissez-faire," and "aggressive vs. laid back." My purpose is not to describe "investor types," of which you are certainly well aware, but it is important for you to understand what "type" each of your clients is in order to serve them best.

Instead, I want to describe toxic personality traits inherent in some of the personalities of people you choose to accept and retain as clients. With many of your clients—or potential clients—your own personality will dovetail nicely and you can work with them, but with others there will definitely be discord and you must make hard decisions about taking on or retaining such clients.

TOXIC PERSONALITIES TO AVOID

Undoubtedly, you will frequently meet potential clients with toxic personality traits hiding behind a veneer of "niceness," waiting for you to take them on, and many may be *high-value* potential clients, thus tempting you to ignore the warning signs. My goal is to help you recognize toxic traits hiding behind that veneer and make hard decisions about whether it is in your best interest to take on or decline to work with such people.

Just as important is recognizing when your gut tells you that a *current* client is toxic to you, so that you can have the courage to cut this person loose and refer him elsewhere.

The variety of toxic personality traits is lengthy and diverse. You will probably even discover some of these toxic traits in your own life among your relatives and friends. I'm not advising you to "get rid" of those folks, but be on the alert so you can "govern yourself accordingly" and try not to get overwhelmed or manipulated by them.

Teaching you specific skills for dealing with each of these "types" is beyond the scope of this book. A wonderful book on the subject that I highly recommend is *Toxic People* by Lillian Glass (1995). Dr. Glass gives insight into the personality dynamics of the people with whom you interact—in both your business and in your life—and she gives skills for dealing with each type.

For our purposes, I will describe 10 common, toxic personality traits that you are likely to encounter in your business, along with brief descriptions. Because you will rarely recognize such traits prior to accepting these clients, it is highly likely that you already have such clients in your practice. I strongly encourage you to eliminate these clients as soon as you become aware of their toxicity and how they affect you. Rationalizing that you can handle such clients or naïvely believing that they will change after spending time with you is an exercise in futility—*and* added stress!

$ THE ABUSIVE (OR ABRASIVE) ALAN

These are hostile, disrespectful people who keep others at a distance with their abusive, insulting "candor." They don't use diplomacy in communicating and believe that being direct and "telling it like it is" all of the time is a virtue. They seem to thrive on provoking and bullying people in a seemingly desperate need to show how smart they are (Glass, 1995, p. 84). They feel powerful by putting down other powerful people (e.g., their wise financial advisor).

Since this is often a high-value client, he believes you will continue to take whatever he dishes out. Can you afford to be constantly provoked by a client who has a chip on his shoulder from childhood and will act out a lifetime of insecurity trying to bully and belittle you?

$ THE CONTROLLING CONNIE

Control freaks tend to be all-or-nothing thinkers, fearing that if they are not in control of everything, they will lose it all. So they hire you to manage their wealth but micro-manage *you*, wanting to take part in and question every decision you make. It's impossible for them to delegate complete responsibility to you, and they believe in maintaining an active role in all that you do within their portfolio. Can you handle having a client who questions every move you make, worries about every dip in the market, and obsessively questions most of your decisions?

$ THE EDDIE HASKELL

If you are in your late 50s or in your 60s, you undoubtedly remember this fictional character on *Leave It to Beaver*, the popular 1950s TV show. Eddie was a classic example of a passive-aggressive, toxic personality. This type of person tries to curry favor with you by slyly complimenting you, hiding his shallow, sneaky character and hostility behind a veneer of "kindness." His main agenda is manipulation while trying not to be obvious about it. If he slips and lets his hostility out, he covers himself by exclaiming, "I was just kidding."

These people are phony, "kissing up to anyone who can do them any good" (Glass, 1995, p. 105). *Their* needs always take priority over yours. You obviously can't trust such an individual and what he says. How will you ever be able to get an accurate feel for this client's needs and concerns if he is a phony with you while maintaining a hidden agenda?

$ THE GLOOM-AND-DOOM DEBBIE

We all know people who constantly bemoan their "fate" and predict bad things happening to them and their money. These pessimistic people always feel like victims of bad luck and constantly worry that bad things will continue to happen to them. If there are two ways to look at a situation, they always choose the negative way. In their catastrophic thinking patterns, they are filled with "what ifs." Any good news you give them about their financial situation will be quickly shut out by the first negative thought that comes into their mind. You show them how well an investment turned out and they respond with a "Yeah, but…" In spite of your positive outlook, they believe it's inevitable that something terrible will happen to their portfolio. Is it worth it to be dragged down by the heavy, negative energy of such clients?

$ THE HIGH-MAINTENANCE MARTY

This type of client needs to be hand-held through every decision in order to feel safe and secure. He embraces a serious lack of self-esteem and rarely feels secure. This client will become very dependent on you for constant reassurance, and he will call regularly to see what decisions you have made in managing his accounts. This can bleed over into much more than your role as his financial advisor. Soon he may depend on you to help him make everyday decisions, etc. He will look to you as his mentor, confidante, or counselor. Can you afford to spend the time you will need to manage such a needy client?

$ THE HISTRIONIC HARRIET

This client has been rewarded in life because of the attention she gets with her dramatic, emotional, overreacting behavior. Because she often exhibits narcissistic qualities as well (see The Narcissistic Ned, below), you will feel exhausted trying to accommodate her.

If you have clients who are actors, on-camera personalities, or celebrities, you know this type. In their profession, they are praised and rewarded for exhibiting this behavior, but this becomes part of their persona and these behaviors weave into all of their interactions. While they are often viewed as charismatic, fun, lively, and interesting, they become "over the top" when they don't feel as if they are getting the attention they demand. They often get frustrated or irritated with situations that involve delayed gratification because they crave it instantly. This makes them very difficult to deal with during down markets, for example. Can you afford to have this drama in your practice?

$ THE NARCISSISTIC NED

This client is an elitist and exists to be admired and adored. He is so wrapped up in himself that he considers himself to be your most important client, demanding your attention whenever he wants it. Since he feels entitled (perhaps by the amount of fees he pays you), he may complain to your assistant that he needs to speak with *you*, and your assistant should interrupt you to take his call.

Also coming from a foundation of insecurity, these people spend their lives looking for attention and accolades from everyone they meet. The advent of Facebook was a boon for them. They fill their Facebook entries with self-aggrandizing dribble. They may flatter you by telling everyone that they have "the best advisor," but they also let everyone know how much *you* adore *them*. Do you have the patience and wherewithal to give this energy-zapping client the time and constant praise he demands?

$ THE OCD OLIVIA

These people are constantly anxious and attempt to moderate that anxiety by controlling every possible detail. This affects their interpersonal skills, and they (often unconsciously) try to control conversations and have difficulty delegating decision making to anyone else. What is really frustrating is that they are so concerned with being perfect and not making mistakes that they ruminate for hours over decisions. Often over-conscientious, scrupulous, and inflexible, this client is very difficult to work with and you will experience great difficulty getting her to make a decision. Moreover, when you seek her approval for a strategy you are considering with regard to her financial plan, you may have to go into excruciating detail with her because of her fear of committing to the "wrong" answer. Can you afford the frustration that comes with dealing with this type of client?

$ THE TYPE-A TED

You learned about Type-A personality traits in Chapter 4, and you, yourself, may very well be a Type-A person. This, of course, is not necessarily toxic, but in its extreme can cause you much stress because of your own need for perfection and control, etc. Since so many successful people maintain Type-A characteristics, I predict that a large percentage of your clients fall into this category. Believing they are as smart as you, this client may second guess your investment strategy and recommendations.

Having similar personalities, your own idiosyncratic traits may clash with theirs, creating difficulties. For example, you may find yourself fighting over control and you both may be impatient with each other. Can you maintain control over and satisfy such clients?

$ THE WISHY-WASHY WANDA

Constantly worried about making a mistake, this type of client vacillates back and forth regarding any financial decision you need her to make. Indecisiveness is the key to her sad existence. An extreme people-pleaser (recall the description in Chapter 4), she tries to determine what *you* want her to say, rather than tell you how she really feels. She doesn't want to offend you or have you judge her negatively.

These clients are unhappy people because they rarely get their needs taken care of; instead, they spend all of their energy pleasing others, including you. Actually this may be an easy client for you to work with because she will go along with anything you suggest, but if you need to know her true wishes, you could get burned. This is another type of client you can't really trust. She is chronically unhappy, hiding, or not trusting her true feelings. Can you afford to retain such a client?

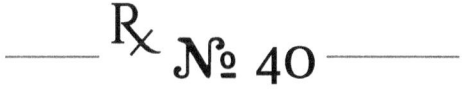

Understand the basic personality traits of toxic people. If you see these traits in your clients and they are causing you stress, eliminate them from your practice.

HOW TO ELIMINATE TOXIC PEOPLE FROM YOUR PRACTICE

Now that you have a basic understanding of toxic personality traits, what can you do if you discover that one or more of your existing clients fits into one of these categories? Ask yourself some simple questions and *be honest* with your responses. First, decide if this client is causing you stress. Do you dread it when your assistant tells you this client is on the line? Do you feel anxious when you have an in-person portfolio review or strategy session scheduled with this client? If you thought your income wouldn't significantly change, would you want to get this client out of your practice?

Certainly, if you answered "yes" to any of these questions, you must eliminate this client. The reduction in stress, along with the rise in your feelings of self-worth, is surely worth whatever temporary loss in income that entails. Plus, with less stress and worry, you are in a much better emotional condition to prospect for new clients with whom you are compatible to replace the loss of income.

To justify eliminating high-value clients from your practice because of the stress and aggravation they cause you may seem very difficult. However, I really like Nick Murray's (2008) advice in this regard:

> Every year on your birthday, give yourself the priceless gift of self-esteem: fire your biggest PITA (an acronym, of course, for Pain In The A**). This is the person who has given you, since your last birthday, the most trouble—however you choose to define "trouble"—which could be anything from paperwork problems to fee carping, to second-guessing your investment recommendations, to just making your skin crawl when you hear his (or her) voice (p. 257).

Murray's point is that you'll give yourself a wonderful birthday present each year by getting rid of the biggest pain in your practice. Moreover, he strongly suggests holding back your frustration and rage, dismissing the client using grace, class, and style. See the sample letter he offers on page 256 of his book (2008)—it closes the door for you and salvages your self-esteem, which will do much more for your success than the client's fees ever did.

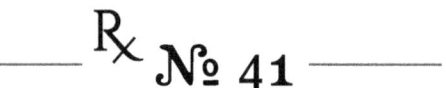

Avoid negative people, and if you cannot avoid them altogether, let their negative messages and feedback about you go in one ear and out the other. Notice the good things you love about the people in your life, and ignore the things you don't love about them. Make sure there are happy, fun-loving people in your life, and stay away from bitter, disgruntled people.

STICK TO YOUR CORE VALUES AS AN ADVISOR

Hopefully, you now value yourself enough that you will never tolerate toxic people in your practice (or, if possible, in your life). Besides valuing *yourself*, you have developed a set of core values regarding your beliefs concerning investment and wealth management/enhancement strategies for your clients. This set of values has been developed and nurtured by your continued education, various mentors you learned from and modeled, specific experiences you have had in your advising profession, and the philosophies of wealth management companies for which you have worked.

If you're wondering why I am including a section on your core investment and wealth management/enhancement values in a book about stress mastery, it's because the stress comes into play when you find yourself either wavering from those values to accommodate the idiosyncrasies or demands of some of your clients, or questioning yourself about those values without a logical reason to do so.

Here is an example of what I mean:

David, one of the advisors whose story appears in this chapter, ascribes to Nick Murray's (2008) core philosophy that advisors best serve their clients by helping them to *modify their emotions and behaviors,* relative to investment and wealth management/enhancement strategies. This involves David's working in the right brain where emotions reside, rather than being a left brained "portfolio-centric" advisor, as Murray describes it. Successful advising for David involves understanding his clients' emotional vulnerabilities as they relate to investment decisions and modifying their behaviors in accordance with David's core values. A large part of this involves educating his clients via his extremely comprehensive weekly commentaries, which he emails to all of his clients.

Let's say that among his many clients, David has some who maintain investment values that do *not* resonate well with David's core values. For example, some of these clients may expect him to predict with accuracy the flows and ebbs of the market, and accordingly, to determine the best time to buy and sell equities for them.

You can envision a conflict when it comes to trying to "accommodate" these clients: On the one hand, David may be firmly opposed to their philosophy of investing and protecting/growing their wealth; on the other hand, he may not want to lose their business. This is where the stress comes in. Does he try to educate them about why he doesn't ascribe to their investment philosophy, but winds up accommodating their wishes against his better judgment in order to "keep them happy"? The stress of becoming a market prognosticator and recommending investments according to his "predictions" is alien to his core wealth management/enhancement values.

There is a term in psychology that refers to the stress that results from your having a set of beliefs or values that directly contradicts your behaviors—it's called "cognitive dissonance." When there is such a discrepancy, something must change in order to reduce your dissonance and keep your stress levels manageable.

David's solution is to stay true to his core values and to educate his clients through his individual interactions with them and his weekly commentaries. David has granted me permission to share with you a sample of this client education process, via a recent weekly commentary during a market rally. You'll be able to decipher his core values in these samples:

> Investors are understandably prone to behavioral mistakes goaded by massive misinformation generated by market fear and euphoria. This is where professional, judicious advice to protect investors from doing permanent damage to their portfolios, as well as grow their financial wealth, provides the greatest service …
>
> My thesis is very simple: Even when markets are doing well, the more one's return relies on the entire market going higher, the greater their losses will be in inevitable market downturns. And when losses during downturns reach a certain level of discomfort, investors are even more prone to behavioral mistakes that turn temporary fluctuations into permanent losses, or psychologically increasing the likelihood that investors will not fall prey to behavioral errors when such downturns do come …
>
> I will do my best, study meticulously, and most of all, maintain my unchangeable belief that timing and selection will never, ever create an investor's desired outcomes—temperament, discipline, and wisdom will …
>
> I would rather lose a client doing the right thing than have a client be happy because I did the wrong thing. So, the first step is to see where my various challenges need intensive perspective, data, and research (which are all solvable problems), vs. the challenges that are already answered, non-emotionally in my core belief system.

If you find that despite giving a client your sage advice and providing the research that validates such advice, that client is still not on the same page with you, then politely and diplomatically tell her that your investment/wealth management values are not in sync with hers. Consequently, for both her sake and yours, you would like to refer her elsewhere, to an advisor who shares her particular investing strategies. As with toxic clients, this is often difficult and perhaps even scary, both because it may be difficult to assert yourself with such clients and because you worry about the loss of their business. My position is that you *need* to refer such rigid clients elsewhere, in order to preserve your sanity!

℞ № 42

Understand your core values regarding investment and wealth management/ enhancement strategies for your clients and stick to them, despite temptations to compromise them in order to please a client.

There are many books written about attracting clients and keeping them in your practice (e.g., Sofia, et al, 2011). While that topic goes beyond the purpose of this book, I would like to address a frequently overlooked aspect of growing your book of business.

HOW TO ATTRACT FEMALE CLIENTS INTO YOUR PRACTICE AND KEEP THEM LOYAL

Obviously, a great source of stress for most advisors involves growing their business through new referrals. As Nick Murray (2008) puts it, every advisory practice begins to die at the point where the advisor becomes "too old, too busy, too tired, and/or too bored to prospect any more" (p. 19).

That being said, I believe that many advisors ignore an often overlooked, lucrative, and underserved segment of potential clients looking for advisors to help them—women. A recent study reported by Fidelity Investments (2013) found that a remarkable 70 percent of widows fire their financial advisors within one year after their spouses die. Why would so many women dismiss the advisor who worked so diligently for their family, in many cases, for years? Why wouldn't they be loyal to that advisor?

The answer is enlightening. When my father died, I recall my mother telling me that she had no idea whether she was left with enough financial recourses to feel secure for the rest of her life. My father had the same advisor ever since they were married, but my mother rarely met with him, or even spoke to him regarding their financial situation. My dad, more or less, told my mother that he would "handle all of that." Mom never understood finances because my dad never educated her in this regard. Consequently, when my dad died, my mother felt extremely worried and insecure, and I had to constantly reassure her about her finances after serving as the middleman between her and her advisor.

This, of course, is not an isolated case. Women often complain that their family advisor is condescending toward them, often meeting only with their spouses or, in joint meetings, having eye contact and communication directed primarily at the man, as if the woman has no say or interest in the financial security of the family. In short, new widows often express a history of being overlooked and undervalued by their family's advisor, leading to a lack of trust in him.

With a successful practice and pipeline to new clients, you might ask yourself why you need to be concerned about female clients in particular. Besides the obvious ethical reasons, some very important statistics about these underserved clients should enlighten you (these are from studies cited and referenced by Holly Buchanan in her book, *Selling Financial Services to Women* (2011) and by Kathleen Burns Kingsbury in her book, *How to Give Financial Advice to Women* (2013):

- 💲 Over the next few decades, it's predicted that women will inherit close to 30 trillion dollars in intergenerational wealth transfers. Because women are likely to outlive their husbands, women will control most of this wealth; plus, they will inherit their parents' wealth.

- 💲 Currently, 57 percent of college graduates are women, and they control more than 60 percent of the personal wealth in the U.S.

- 💲 22 percent of women currently earn more money than their spouses.

- 💲 Women make approximately 80 percent of their families' buying decisions.

- 💲 Women control 89 percent of currently existing bank accounts.

- 💲 28 percent of homeowners are single women.

- 💲 45 percent of the millionaires in the U.S. are women.

- 💲 In 2009, 40 percent of private companies were at least 50 percent owned by women, compared with only 26 percent of companies in 1997 in that category.

- 💲 Women currently own 20 percent of firms with revenue of at least $1 million.

℞ № 43

Build into your prospecting plan the goal of soliciting more female clients, and be proactive in dealing with the female (and spouses of male) clients you have currently. Have meetings with female spouses <u>alone</u>, in order to understand their unique concerns. Make it safe for them to discuss issues, which they may not relate to you in a joint meeting with their spouse.

In short, women are earning more, inheriting more, and controlling more wealth than ever before. This is a huge, untapped source of new clients awaiting every financial advisor, *if* he understands some key points about the mindset of women, their needs, and their desires.

In the next chapter you will read about Karen, a remarkable female advisor who has enjoyed a very successful career for more than 20 years. But I also want to highlight her career here because her practice caters exclusively to female clients. Karen hires *only* female advisors to join her practice, primarily because she believes they are "best suited" to work with female clients. Aware of the statistics cited above about women and their wealth, she decided many years ago that focusing on female clients would be a very wise way to build her practice. And boy (or girl), was she right!

When she was in her teens, Karen—much like me—observed her mother making virtually none of the financial decisions in the family, almost as if that wasn't her role. Furthermore, her father rarely shared financial decisions, insurance plans, or any form of estate planning with her mother. Consequently, when Karen's father died, her mother was frozen with feelings of helplessness, not understanding the details or nuances of her financial situation, thus feeling very anxious, insecure, and frightened.

Because of this history in her own family, Karen decided early on that she would immerse herself in a career that would serve women in this regard. Karen vowed that her clients would never find themselves in her mother's position. (The rest of Karen's story will be found in Chapter 8.)

As an aside, when I was a psychologist in the U.S. Air Force during the Vietnam war, one of my duties was helping the wives and families of servicemen killed, captured, or missing in the war. I was shocked at the high percentage of women who had absolutely no idea about any of the financial plans or arrangements that their spouses had prepared before departing on their tour of duty. Most didn't even know where to find the paperwork or the names of insurance companies or brokerage firms with whom their spouses worked.

WHY WOMEN BECOME DISENCHANTED WITH THEIR ADVISORS

Getting back to the dramatic statistic that 70 percent of widows dismiss their families' advisors within the first year after their spouses' deaths, it's important to understand why this occurs. Women leave their advisors and hire the competition not because of disappointment over investment performance, but because they feel "misunderstood, unheard, or overlooked (Kingsbury, 2013, p. 3)." From my interviews with advisors who have worked with women who fired their old advisors, the predominating reasons they left are condensed in comments like these:

- $ "He didn't listen to me."
- $ "He was condescending toward me."
- $ "He hardly looked at me or asked my opinion."
- $ "I couldn't trust him to consider my needs."

- $ "I felt overlooked and undervalued."
- $ "I didn't believe he really understood my fears and goals."

What's more, for some male advisors, the problem of dealing appropriately with female clients may be part of a larger issue—dealing with women in general. Sometimes males buy into stereotypical views of women and finances, such as believing the following myths:

- $ Women prefer to leave financial decisions to men.
- $ Women are too emotional and base financial decisions on their emotions at the time.
- $ Women are impulsive and may make financial decisions they later regret.

If you maintain any of these beliefs about women, unless you plan to engage in therapy or gender sensitivity training, then perhaps working with female clients is *not* something you should consider.

WOMEN'S FINANCIAL FEARS AND UNMET NEEDS IN THE FINANCIAL ARENA

You've probably heard that money problems are one of the most significant factors leading to divorce. Dr. Sonya Britt, an assistant professor in the Institute of Financial Planning at Kansas State University, collected interview data from 4,500 couples who had gone through divorce, and the data showed definitively that the #1 factor in causing their divorces was money issues (Britt, 2013). Many couples avoid dealing with financial issues, as if it is a taboo subject, with women often leaving financial decisions to the males in their lives in order to avoid controversy.

Recently, Allianz Life reported the results of an eye-opening study they conducted (The 2013 Women, Money & Power Study), where they surveyed more than 2,200 women between the ages of 25 and 75 with a minimum household income of $30,000 per year. Several remarkable discoveries emerged:

- $ Large percentages of these women continue to feel uncomfortable dealing with financial issues, but at the same time believe they *need* to take an active part in managing their money.
- $ Two-thirds of married women are concerned about leaving all of their financial decisions to their spouses, and 57 percent say they handle major investment decisions and retirement planning themselves.

- $ Women across all the demographics exhibit a surprising, irrational fear regarding finances: Almost 50 percent of the women surveyed fear losing all of their money and becoming homeless. Even a third of the highest earners ($200,000+) have the same fear. The authors suggest that this points to a deeply held type of financial insecurity that is not an issue with males, in general.

- $ 57 percent of married women say that fear of their spouse dying is a primary fear that keeps them awake at night, but fear of running out of money is a close second.

Perhaps because of their fears and unmet needs regarding financial security, women generally perceive that the financial advising industry is oriented more toward serving men. Large percentages of these survey respondents feel alienated by this industry, and 62 percent of women express an interest in learning more about finances and retirement planning, yet *the same percentage of women presently do not have a financial advisor!* Many view the Internet as the most reliable source for making financial decisions. So, a huge opportunity is presenting itself to educate and help women, who presently command—and will continue to command—a large percentage of the wealth in this country.

HOW YOU CAN CAPITALIZE ON THIS OPPORTUNITY: BEGIN BY LISTENING

> *People will forget what you said, they will forget what you did,*
> *but they will never forget how you made them feel.*
>
> —MAYA ANGELOU, AMERICAN AUTHOR AND POET

Financial professionals must understand that women need to feel *genuinely* cared about and valued in any relationship, including the relationship with their financial advisor. As someone once said, "Most people don't care about how much you know until they know how much you care."

Feeling cared about far outweighs the details about what happens or what specific decisions are made in those relationships. Women want their needs and fears to be listened to and understood by the advisor they choose in order to help them feel secure. "While most women do not have a gender preference in working with a financial advisor, research shows that many women have a strong preference in the way they receive financial advice," said Alexandra Taussig, senior vice president of National Financial®, a Fidelity Investments company (Fidelity Investments, 2013a). Advisors who recognize this and hone their communication strategies with both their male and female clients may have a significant opportunity to grow their businesses.

Married women want to build a *genuine relationship* with their advisor, feel like they are treated as an equal partner to their spouse by the advisor, attend all meetings that their spouse attends, have some one-on-one meetings with the advisor without their spouse present, and focus on investments that address *their* needs, as well as those of their partners.

In order to trust you, women in general—married or not—must be *genuinely listened to*. I teach all of my advisor clients the skill of "active listening" to effectively communicate with their clients, especially women. While the specifics of active listening are described in Chapter 4, here are some additional tips.

Prior to meeting with a female client, tell your secretary to be sure to hold all calls, etc., and turn off your cell phone. Come out from behind your desk and invite her to sit in close proximity during the meeting. Make sure you make and maintain good eye contact with her throughout the visit.

The key to active listening is *not* concerning yourself with what you will say next or how to respond to the speaker's comments or questions. Instead, you pay particular attention to *what* she says—her tone and nonverbal communication (facial gestures, body language, eye contact, etc.)—in order to put yourself in her shoes and understand the essence of her concerns.

You then paraphrase what she said by mirroring it back to her and empathizing with her concerns *from her perspective* (even if you think they are irrational), because you must show that you truly understand her concerns before judging them or responding to them with your opinion. So, let's say she tells you she is afraid that when her husband dies she will not have enough money to hold onto her home, that she'll be forced to move into a tiny apartment, and that she'll consequently be miserable and alone for the rest of her life.

Even if your knowledge of her financial situation and the long-term plan put into place by her husband suggests that her fears are unwarranted and irrational, this is *not* the time for making such a response. Do not give your views or thoughts about what she is saying until you are certain you understand her fears *from her perspective* and she confirms that you "get it." Often the first visit is just you listening and understanding—not giving advice to her. An appropriate response to this concern might be:

> "I'm hearing from you that you're frightened about your future and in particular, you're worried that your life will be unbearable when your husband dies. You don't know how you'll be able to keep the house and you fear being alone and poor for the rest of your life."

℞ № 44

Review the suggestions for attracting female clients to your practice and accommodating their needs, fears, and goals. Then practice the active-listening skills you are working on with all prospective and active clients, especially female.

There are several more steps in the active-listening process, and I have written many articles on this subject (e.g., Singer, 2012.) Since active listening is such an important skill to master, I will provide another example here, as described by Kathleen Burns Kingsbury in her wonderful book, *How to Give Financial Advice to Women*. Here are a few highlights:

STEP 1:

Lead with an open-ended question to begin the dialogue. For example, you might ask your client: "What is your biggest concern right now?" Even if her response has nothing to do with finances, go there with her. Your job is to understand the emotional space she is in now, not necessarily to direct her in the financial arena.

STEP 2:

Ask clarifying questions to get an in-depth understanding of her concerns and needs. For example, "What are your greatest fears about what will happen to your financial situation over the next five years or so?"

STEP 3:

This is the key to active listening, as I emphasized above. Reflect back (paraphrase) what you just heard, in your own words. For example, if she said, "I don't know how to raise my children without their father in the picture, and I'm afraid I can't handle it alone," you could paraphrase that with, "What I'm hearing you say is you're worried that without your husband, you'll have difficulty raising your children, and that feels overwhelming and scary right now. Is that how you feel?"

STEP 4:

Ask for more clarification. For example, "What specifically are you afraid you won't be able to handle with the children? Is it a financial fear or something else?"

STEP 5:

Summarize both the content and *emotion* of the client's conversation. For example, "It sounds as if you're feeling *overwhelmed* at the moment, not knowing how you're going to parent the children alone, and you're *afraid* of failing in that regard."

Note that the conversation may go anywhere. Your job is to *listen* and understand your client's concerns. As I mentioned above, initial conversations may never come around to financial issues. It doesn't matter. Your client needs to know that you are concerned, you understand her, and you will help her. Once she understands that you care about her and are a trusted support system for her, helping her to make sound financial decisions will be much easier in future conversations. It all starts with trust and communicating *genuine* concern for her welfare, her family, and their future. This is the *process* of developing trust in you as an advisor … it's not about the *outcome* (e.g., which products or investments she will purchase at this time).

ADDITIONAL WAYS TO SOLICIT AND ACCOMMODATE FEMALE CLIENTS

- $ Review your book of business, determine what percentage of your clients is female, and assess whether you have been accommodating your current female clients adequately and whether you should focus your prospecting on attaining more female clients.
- $ Write investment-related articles for your local newspaper or broker dealer publication that address female issues and concerns.
- $ Make sure your office staff reflects your values as they pertain to soliciting female clients to your practice and developing their trust.
- $ When meeting a new couple, schedule separate meetings with the husband and wife to give her an opportunity to share her concerns and desires with you, confidentially and without her husband's dominating the conversation.
- $ Offer to speak at meetings of female-owned businesses.
- $ Sponsor a female-oriented charity or client appreciation event.
- $ Volunteer your time at widow and divorce workshops.
- $ Build a referral network among family law attorneys—especially female attorneys—showing them the special care and attention you provide to your female clientele.
- $ Always remember that women are about relationships and trust, so be sure to keep these values paramount as you work with them.

An advisor who "gets it" in terms of attracting ideal clients to his practice is Marty. Marty has been advising clients since 1976, and he attributes much of his success to targeting "ideal clients" by using a third-party resource. This system filters prospects using 70 demographic, financial, and psychographic traits, giving Marty a list of those candidates with the best fit for his practice. Marty uses this list to decide which clients he will solicit.

Because Marty also understands the dynamic between male advisors and female clients, he insists that married male clients bring their spouses to every meeting, and Marty engages those spouses with the same listening skills he uses with the males.

Marty believes what differentiates him from most advisors is that he makes sure he connects with each client at least 100 times a year. He accomplishes this through weekly updates via email, a monthly client newsletter, and messages from his entire team constantly going out to his clients. Indeed, Marty understands how to select ideal clients for his practice, and he strives to make them feel more comfortable about their financial decisions.

Now, back to our other highly successful advisor, David. He, too, surrounds himself with a high-quality team of proficient support people; but each client/family is also carefully attended to personally by David in order to assess and plan for their financial needs, goals, and aspirations. His firm is a comprehensive one, with estate and legacy planning as well as tax planning included in the services provided to clients.

David insists on face-to-face, periodic meetings with each client/family to be sure all clients' needs are heard and that they are on board with David's plan. As I noted above, in addition to an annual Client Appreciation Event, David writes a powerful Weekly Commentary (see the samples of comments earlier in this chapter) that he emails to every client. David avoids a lot of stressful calls from inquisitive and often frantic clients by proactively sending out this commentary each week. The commentaries include David's personal, learned, and respected take on the financial events of the week, as well as candid answers to highly sophisticated questions that David fashions by anticipating concerns and issues that would be of interest to all clients.

But how does David deal with his on-the-job stressors?

Shaping and educating his team to embrace his core values and delegating responsibilities has taken much of David's stress away. In addition, he "forces" himself to exercise and take personal time, as well as spend quality time with his family.

David's biggest stressor in the past has been dealing with toxic clients—particularly the "Abusive Alans" and "High-Maintenance Martys." After years of taking on virtually every client who chose to work with him, David recognized that he had relinquished much control in his client relationships because of his fear of turning away or losing business.

Regarding "Abusive Alans," David says that these clients caused him much more stress than even the 2008 financial crisis did! Like Nick Murray's (2008) philosophy, David believes that advisors need to "value themselves enough to *not* keep such people on their client rosters" (private conversation with David, 2014). As an example, after much internal debate, David finally dismissed a high-net-worth, abusive client. Once he did so, he not only felt relief from the stress involved in dealing with that person, but a sense of peace and "liberating self-esteem" embraced him. Remarkably, the relief plus renewed energy he felt led to a record year, despite having removed that high-net-worth client from his book of business.

As you read earlier in this chapter, "High-Maintenance Martys" are insecure and demand a tremendous amount of attention, time, and reassurance. They can be like an anchor around your neck and when you do give them kind attention, it serves to reinforce their dependency on you. Consequently, when David senses such toxic traits, he refers these clients out of his practice.

Since "High Maintenance Martys" are typically nice people and get offended easily, they must be treated gently. Moving them to another team member or referring them out has really paid off for David. He firmly believes that eliminating this type of energy-draining client has also opened up more time for him, giving him peace of mind and more energy to get other things accomplished. Accordingly, he has been able to devote more time and energy to clients with whom he enjoys harmony, and as predicted, his revenues and referrals grew rapidly after eliminating those clients from his practice.

This is yet another example of the inverse relationship between stress levels and revenues generated. Yet so many advisors will not pull the trigger on such clients because they're locked in on the lost revenue that referring a client will cost them, instead of looking at the big picture and realizing that this will actually lead to *increased* revenues.

As I mentioned, David remains forever true to his core values and continually educates his clients about his rationale for adopting and maintaining these values. He will also recommend that a client with needs or desires that conflict with his values move on to an advisor where his or her needs can be better served. Such courage has served David well in terms of avoiding more stress.

Remarkably, in order to remain sharp and not miss anything that could improve his services even more, David maintains a Client Advisory Board. This consists of biannual meetings with high-value clients in order to get objective feedback about how he and his team are doing, and he solicits suggestions for improvement. In addition, David encourages ad hoc email interchanges whenever any client has questions or comments.

David's courage and foresight serves his clients, team, and himself very well during these challenging economic times. His practice is highly efficient and growing, yet every client feels special.

ACTION PLAN FOR STRESS MASTERY

Table 7.1 My Action Plan for Stress Mastery

Check each one when you've accomplished it. Feel free to add additional new behaviors in the spaces provided.

New Behavior	What I Did and the Date Accomplished
☐ I will make a list of the clients who cause me the most stress and make note of personality traits that fit the toxic definitions. ☐ ☐ ☐	What I did: Date accomplished:
☐ I will use tactful communications to refer these clients out of my practice. ☐ ☐ ☐	What I did: Date accomplished:
☐ I will focus attention on how I solicit and communicate with prospective female clients. ☐ ☐ ☐	What I did: Date accomplished:

(continued)

Table 7.1 MY ACTION PLAN FOR STRESS MASTERY (CONT.)

☐ I will be sensitive to the needs of female clients. ☐ ☐ ☐	What I did:
	Date accomplished:
☐ I will consider new ways to solicit female clients into my practice. ☐ ☐ ☐	What I did:
	Date accomplished:
☐ I will write down my core values as they apply to investment and wealth management/enhancement strategies for my clients. ☐ ☐ ☐	What I did:
	Date accomplished:
☐ Where there are major discrepancies between my values and those of a client, I will determine how much stress that causes to me and if it is significant, I will use tactful communications to refer that client out of my practice. ☐ ☐ ☐	What I did:
	Date accomplished:

8

HOW *to* BECOME *and* REMAIN A RESILIENT PERSON

A pessimist is one who makes difficulties of his opportunities; an optimist is one who makes opportunities of his difficulties.

—REGINALD B. MANSELL, AUTHOR

LEARNING OBJECTIVES

+ I will understand the specific characteristics of optimistic and pessimistic interpretations of events in my life.

+ I will understand the relationship between events in my life, my interpretation of those events, and ultimately, my vulnerability to disease.

+ I will be able to use the A-B-C-D-E model for developing optimistic thinking.

+ I will be able to use the Thinking-Pattern Worksheet (TPW) to convert pessimistic thinking to optimistic thinking.

+ I will learn many additional stress buffers that I will incorporate into my ongoing efforts to build resilience.

Congratulations! You are almost finished learning how to master the stresses in your life. By now, you must be very optimistic that you can turn the corner, take charge of your life, and begin to feel consistently better. But in case there is still a glimmer of self-doubt remaining, let's learn about how to boost your optimism, or if you are a pessimist, learn how to turn that kind of negative thinking around quickly. A large part of remaining resilient in the face of stressful situations is having an *optimistic* attitude.

Recall that I mentioned Karen in the last chapter. I chose the story of Karen to close out the book because she is an amazing example of a resilient person who has successfully inoculated herself from stress. Karen has bounced back from several setbacks, disposed of her "internal critic," overcome many life stressors, disregarded negative opinions from others, committed herself to accomplishing her goals, and remained optimistic in her dream of becoming a very successful advisor, not just financially, but in the service of all her clients.

A life-changing opportunity for Karen took place when she was only 16. She was given a job in a nursing home where she was paid to simply sit and listen to the residents. She was instructed to help the residents to feel safe and important by *listening* to their concerns and fears.

When Karen began working as a financial advisor, she worked for male-dominated firms and was saddened watching her advisor colleagues sell products and equities to their clients (particularly female clients) without really listening to the clients' concerns. Karen believed that something important was missing in those advisor-client relationships..

In her view, an advisor could be holistic and offer many services to clients (e.g., estate, legacy, and tax planning). She read research showing that female clients, in particular, were being underserved or poorly served, mostly by male advisors. She came to believe that a fee-for-service model would serve both herself and her clients better.

Karen's family, friends, and colleagues never bought into her model for success. She was told that a fee-based business would not be feasible in a brokers' world. Incidentally, she was doing all of this after undergoing a divorce and raising three children as a single parent—key life events that can quickly pile up stress as you discovered in Chapter 2.

Nevertheless, Karen spent as much time as she could focusing on relationship building and really *listening* to current and prospective clients. She believed she could find a niche with these people and develop a thriving business. She was convinced that just as in the nursing home, she would be trusted if she listened to people's concerns and needs. Once Karen understood those concerns and needs, she could make recommendations for products and services specifically tailored for those clients' situations.

Karen also recognized the importance of treating her employees with the same care and respect as her clients. She knew she could not ask her employees to be extraordinary; they had to choose to be extraordinary, and having her as a role model helped them feel valued and appreciated. In her words: "People don't care what you do or how you do it. They only care about why you do it." So the values that Karen brought to her practice, she brought to her staff. In short, she walked her talk in the office.

By now you know that each case I present turns out well. How well did it turn out for Karen? You know the drill. Finish the chapter and you'll discover the answer.

LEARNING TO BECOME OPTIMISTIC

> *Quit now, you'll never make it. If you disregard this advice, you'll be halfway there.*
>
> —DAVID ZUCKER, FILM DIRECTOR

Let's begin with some definitions. Looking at the glass as half empty or half full doesn't give you the whole story of optimism vs. pessimism, although there is some validity to that commonly used definition. Optimism and pessimism are really about how you interpret or explain bad and good events that take place in your life and your expectations about whether those kinds of events will continue to occur (Seligman, 1998).

As you can see summarized in Table 8.1 on the next page, *optimists* explain that bad things take place in their lives because of *external* factors, representing *isolated* and *temporary* setbacks, unlikely to be repeated and not their fault. Circumstances beyond their control, bad luck, and the behaviors of other people may all contribute to this misfortune. Optimists might say to themselves something like, *This was awful but I couldn't do anything about it. It was a fluke, it will probably never happen again, and it won't affect any other part of my life. I'm moving on.*

Because they believe that better days will soon be here, they see misfortune and defeat as *temporary* setbacks and signals to dig in and try harder. This way of interpreting difficult events motivates them to persevere and take charge of their lives to maximize the probability that better days will soon be here.

Table 8.1	CHARACTERISTICS OF OPTIMISTIC AND PESSIMISTIC INTERPRETATIONS

When **Bad** Things Happen	
Optimistic Orientation	**Pessimistic Orientation**
❖ This was a fluke. It's not my style. I had a bad day at the office because I didn't get enough sleep last night. **(external cause)** ❖ I can control the amount of sleep I get and make sure this doesn't happen again. I wasn't as prepared as I should have been before meeting my client and that's why she didn't understand what I was trying to explain to her and got frustrated with me. I'll make sure that doesn't happen next time. **(control)** ❖ This kind of situation is unlikely to repeat itself. I got irritated with my client because she didn't understand me. **(specific and temporary)**	❖ Bad things happen because of my lack of skills; it's my fault. I'll continue to have bad days at the office no matter what I do because I'm not cut out for this occupation. **(internal cause)** ❖ Bad things will continue to happen to me no matter what I do. **(learned helplessness)** ❖ I didn't make a good impression in my meeting with the client because I always screw up these kinds of meetings. ❖ Bad things always happen to me and will continue to happen in many areas of my life. **(hopelessness)** ❖ I lost my cool with that client because I'm impatient and will never be able to deal calmly with dumb clients. **(permanent and pervasive)**

When **Good** Things Happen	
Optimistic Orientation	Pessimistic Orientation
❖ *Good things happened to me because of my skills, effort, and/or motivation. I have a nice book of business because of my knowledge, experience, and excellent advising skills.* **(control)** ❖ *Good things will continue to occur in my career over time. No matter how many difficult clients I have in my practice, I will always be able to manage them with creative solutions for their financial needs or I'll remove them from my practice.* **(permanent)** ❖ *Good things will happen across many aspects of my life.* **(pervasive)** ❖ *Because I'm smart and creative, good things will happen in many aspects of my life.* **(control)**	❖ *This was a fluke. I was just lucky. I was lucky to get into the Million Dollar Round Table because my existing clients' wealth has increased dramatically. It increased because I made a couple of recommendations that could have gone either way.* **(lack of control)** ❖ *This is not likely to happen again. I was just lucky to get some high-value clients into my practice this year, but I doubt it will happen again.* **(temporary)** ❖ *Good things generally won't happen to me. If they do, it's a fluke.* **(specific occurrence)** ❖ *Maybe I do well in my advising career, but my family life and my social life are a mess.* **(lack of control)**

Critics say that such thinking avoids taking responsibility for failure by simply finding excuses and blaming others when one fails. Whether this argument has any credence is irrelevant because such optimistic thinking most often leads to successful outcomes in the future. For decades, researchers have reported these positive outcomes in a diverse array of situations, including helping athletes win after losses, building one's immune system, warding off diseases, and even helping breast cancer victims live longer (Haven, Frandsen, Karren, & Hooker, 1992; Peterson & Bossio, 1993; Seligman, 1998; Siegel, 1998; Sobel & Ornstein, 1996).

On the other hand, when good things happen to optimists, they use the opposite thinking to explain those events. They believe those good outcomes happened precisely because of their own motivation, hard work, and feelings of control. Such good outcomes will repeat themselves many times. After good things happen, they might say to themselves, *This is the way my life goes. Good things always happen to me in all sorts of situations, and it's because I put myself in a position for good things to happen by my work ethic and intelligence*. So, optimists take credit for good outcomes and blame bad outcomes on external factors.

Pessimists, on the other hand, explain unfortunate events that occur in their lives as *chronic* and *permanent* setbacks caused by their own inadequacies, and they therefore expect bad things to happen to them repeatedly. In short, they believe it was their fault that these events turned out the way they did. Consequently, pessimists often feel helpless, hopeless, and trapped in life circumstances they believe are permanent.

Martin Seligman (1998), who is the father of this pioneering research, calls this *learned helplessness*. Pessimists believe they have no control over what happens to them in life, and therefore, whatever they do won't matter.

When good things happen to pessimists, they attribute those outcomes to luck and take no credit for them, thinking: *It doesn't matter what I do; I'll never be successful. On the few occasions when I was successful, I was just lucky.*

Not surprisingly, there is much scientific research showing that people who maintain an optimistic orientation toward life are healthier, suffer fewer catastrophic illnesses, and actually live longer than do pessimists. Seligman (1998), who insists that optimistic thinking can be learned at any age, reports studies in which having an optimistic orientation by age 45 is the primary determinant of a person's health over the next twenty years.

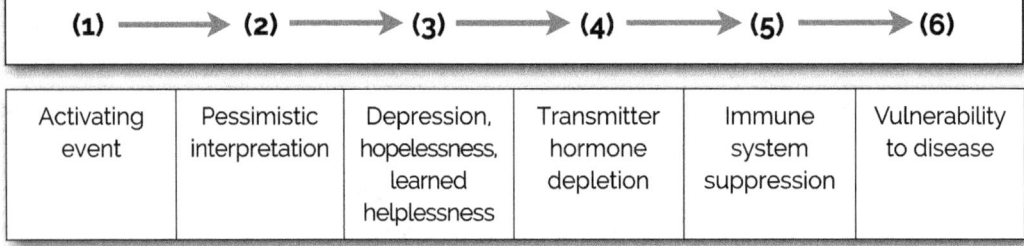

Figure 8.1 THE RELATIONSHIP BETWEEN EVENTS, PESSIMISTIC INTERPRETATIONS, AND DISEASE VULNERABILITY

| Activating event | Pessimistic interpretation | Depression, hopelessness, learned helplessness | Transmitter hormone depletion | Immune system suppression | Vulnerability to disease |

Here's how Seligman (1998) and others (Sapolsky, 1998) explain what happens. As you can see in Figure 8.1, life events and experiences that are interpreted in pessimistic ways lead to the emotional consequences of hopelessness, learned helplessness, and depression (i.e., stress outcomes). In an effort to fight the source of the stress, there is a resultant depletion in nerve-transmission-receptor hormones. This is because your brain doesn't know whether your stress resulted from surgery, childbirth, your life being threatened, dealing with an angry client, or simply from hopeless feelings. Therefore, the pessimistic, helpless, and hopeless feelings you experience as a result of specific events in your life—and the negative, pessimistic way in which you interpret those feelings—produces the same depletion of neurotransmitters that would occur if you had surgery, were injured, avoided prospecting, or dealt with a life-threatening situation.

Recall that the SNS (sympathetic nervous system) switches on whenever you are stressed and have negative, self-defeating thoughts and beliefs, such as hopeless and helpless thoughts.

When the brain recognizes this neurotransmitter depletion, it then suppresses the immune system because in a real emergency, it's not efficient to be working on long-term immunity strengthening; instead, the body works on dealing with the urgent situation. While the immune system is shutting down, the production of disease-killing T-cells shuts down, as well as the production of natural-killer cells, whose purpose is to recognize bacteria, disease inducers, and foreign cells that attempt to invade the body. You can imagine the vulnerability to disease that this shutting down of the immune system leads to.

In summary, when one views events in a pessimistic, helpless, and hopeless way, the emergency system is continuously turned on, thus shutting down the immune system and leading to increased susceptibility to disease. So it's certainly not surprising that countless studies conclude that people who have a *consistently pessimistic* orientation suffer from far more illnesses than do optimists, and optimists also outlive pessimists (Seligman, 1998).

The positive health outcomes for optimistically oriented people have been replicated with a whole host of studies, also reported by Seligman (1998). Although no claim is made that optimism can overcome a terminal (lethal) amount of cancer (although famed author and physician Bernie Siegel (1986, 1998) would argue that such miracles are possible using positive affirmations), Seligman (1998) concludes from the scientific evidence that "Psychological traits, particularly optimism, can produce good health. This evidence makes sense of—and supersedes—the torrent of personal stories in which states ranging from laughter to the will to live appear to help health" (p. 173). In fact, he cites research showing that even when people have an unrealistically optimistic view of their future—such as denying the severity of an illness—this belief structure alone may significantly help them cope and can extend their lives.

We now know that your behaviors are certainly not set in stone. Regardless of your genetic hardwiring, you can learn new, healthier behaviors (the magic 21 days). With practice, optimistic thinking habits can take the place of pessimistic thinking habits. Furthermore, you now know that if you have experienced many stress-causing events in the last 12 months, you have some control over new events affecting you in the coming months by simply delaying them.

Seligman's books (1998, 2002) are filled with methods for building an optimistic explanatory style, both for adults and children. The results of his research show that adults and children alike reduce their risk of depression, boost their self-esteem, and enhance their physical health by practicing the skills he teaches.

Good News!

You have already learned the key elements of changing your thinking from pessimistic to optimistic thinking—review the TPW from Chapter 5.

Figure 8.2	THE A-B-C-D-E MODEL FOR DEVELOPING OPTIMISTIC THINKING

(A) →	(B) →	(C) →	(D) →	(E)
Activating event (stress causing)	Negative beliefs about A	Consequent emotions (pessimistic, hopeless, helpless)	Disputing thoughts	Energized emotions (optimistic, hopeful, in control)

The main premise of Seligman's books is learning to use the A-B-C-D-E method of examining stress-inviting events and the resultant negative thoughts. As you saw in Chapter 5, the most important skill to be developed is finding logical rebuttal thoughts that dispute the original pessimistic thoughts. Once you do this, the original negative emotions give way to healthy, energized emotions. (See Figure 8.2.)

R̥ № 45

Using the TPWs in Tables 8.2 and 8.3, practice interpreting unfortunate events in optimistic ways.

The TPW is again the vehicle by which we can learn to identify our distorted-thinking patterns that lead to pessimistic, helpless, and hopeless feelings and dispute them on the spot. The sample TPW on the next page shows the beliefs (thoughts) and the disputed thinking of a pessimistic financial advisor.

It's important to be very adamant about disputing those thoughts. Use your rubber band and shout, "Stop!" to yourself once you recognize you are engaging in negative, pessimistic thoughts. In Table 8.2, for example (see next page), this advisor believes that his business "is a disaster" and he doesn't see how it will ever get better. This is a classic example of *magnification* and blowing the situation out of proportion in his mind. He must dispute such a thought vehemently with a rational rebuttal, such as the following:

There is no need to magnify or blow things out of proportion. I had hoped for a better year, but because of the economy, all advisors have been faced with new challenges in trying to help their clients feel secure. Every advisor feels overwhelmed at times. This is mainly because of the challenges that go with the job, not because of my incompetence. I have the resources to meet these challenges with creative thinking and planning.

Once you realize that it is your pattern of *distorted* beliefs and thoughts (B) about your situation(s) (A) that is the cause of your pessimism and hopeless and helpless feelings (C) (rather than chronic weaknesses within yourself), you can vehemently dispute (D) those beliefs and thoughts, resulting in energized (E), revitalized feelings and emotions and a more optimistic outlook.

When you are in the process of disputing the distorted beliefs, ask yourself the following: *What evidence is there that supports my belief? Are there any alternative explanations for my conclusions? Does holding on to this belief serve any useful purpose?*

A blank TPW is provided for you in Table 8.3. As before, make several copies of this form to use, and use it every time you feel down, stressed, helpless, overwhelmed—and particularly—pessimistic. If you are conscientious about using a TPW every time you begin to feel negative emotions, you will quickly learn how to recognize and dispute the self-talk distortions that have led to your unhappiness and pessimistic attitudes. About how many days will it take of consistently practicing this skill to make a permanent change in your pessimistic views of your life? You guessed it—21 days.

| Table 8.2 | SAMPLE THINKING-PATTERN WORKSHEET (TPW) FOR OPTIMISM |

Description of the activating event (A) that led to his *pessimistic*, emotional reactions:

"I came home from the office today completely drained. I don't like several of my clients, and I don't have patience for their whining about their losses when the market dips."

Negative emotions (C) prior to disputing my thoughts and their intensity (1–10):

1. *I'm feeling overwhelmed, and I don't see how this can ever get better.* (10)
2. *I'm feeling frightened about my future as a financial advisor.* (6)
3. *I feel hopeless and helpless.* (8)

Automatic Thoughts and Beliefs (B)	Self-Defeating Thinking Pattern	Disputing Responses (Rebuttal) (D)
1. *My business is a disaster. I've lost some good clients this year and have not been able to replace them. I'm feeling overwhelmed, and I don't see how this can ever get better.*	**a. Overgeneralization** **b. Magnification**	a. *There is no need to magnify this or blow things out of proportion. I had hoped for a better year, but because of the economy, all advisors have been faced with new challenges in trying to help their clients feel secure. Every advisor feels overwhelmed at times. This is mainly because of the challenges that go with the job, not because of my incompetence. I have the resources to meet these challenges with creative thinking and planning.*

Automatic Thoughts and Beliefs (B)	Self-Defeating Thinking Pattern	Disputing Responses (Rebuttal) (D)
2. I don't think I'll ever be happy in this career.	**a. Fortune-telling** **b. Emotional reasoning**	a. *Does the fact that I lost a few clients during these tumultuous economic times mean that I'll never be successful? I've dealt with adversity before in my life and didn't have to run away. I'll talk to my colleagues about strategies to help our clients during these times.*
3. This is really happening because I don't have what it takes to be a successful financial advisor.	**a. All or nothing** **b. Blaming** **c. Emotional reasoning**	a. *My manager hired me because he saw something in me that he predicted would make me successful, and success is not simply based on dealing with a few weeks of a tumultuous market.*

Negative emotions after rebutting my thoughts and their intensity (1–10):

1. *I'm feeling overwhelmed.* (3)
2. *I'm feeling frightened.* (1)
3. *I feel hopeless and helpless.* (2)
4. _____
5. _____

Self-Defeating Thinking Patterns: *all or nothing; magnification; mind reading; catastrophizing; being right; should, have to, must; control fallacy; overgeneralization; blaming; and emotional reasoning*

Adapted from Matthew McKay and Martha Davis. *Thoughts and Feelings*. 1981, with permission from New Harbinger Press.

Table 8.3	BLANK THINKING-PATTERN WORKSHEET (TPW) FOR OPTIMISM

Make copies of this table before you fill it in so you can fill in the blank spaces every time you feel pessimistic emotions.

Description of the activating event (A) that led to *pessimistic*, emotional reactions:

1. _____
2. _____
3. _____

Negative emotions (C) prior to disputing my thoughts and their intensity (1–10):

1. _____
2. _____
3. _____

Automatic Thoughts and Beliefs (B)	Self-Defeating Thinking Pattern	Disputing Responses (Rebuttal) (D)
1.	a. b.	*1.*
2.	a. b.	*2.*

Automatic Thoughts and Beliefs (B)	Self-Defeating Thinking Pattern	Disputing Responses (Rebuttal) (D)
3.	a. b.	3.
4.	a. b.	4.

If you have more than four thoughts, continue this on another sheet.

Negative emotions after rebutting my thoughts and their intensity (1–10):

1. _____
2. _____
3. _____
4. _____
5. _____

Self-Defeating Thinking Patterns: *all or nothing; magnification; mind reading; catastrophizing; being right; should, have to, must; control fallacy; overgeneralization; blaming; and emotional reasoning*

Adapted from Matthew McKay and Martha Davis. *Thoughts and Feelings.* 1981, with permission from New Harbinger Press.

Perhaps the best example of remaining optimistic in the face of defeat is represented by this gentleman's life. Here is a series of events that befell him:

- $ He failed in business and suffered bankruptcy in 183.
- $ He was defeated in a run for state legislature in 1832.
- $ He failed again in business and again suffered bankruptcy in 1834.
- $ His fiancée died in 1835.
- $ He suffered a nervous breakdown in 1836.
- $ He was again defeated in election in 1838.
- $ He was defeated running for U.S. Congress in 1843.
- $ He was defeated again running for U.S. Congress in 1846.
- $ Once again, he was defeated running for U.S. Congress in 1848.
- $ He was defeated running for U.S. Senate in 1855.
- $ He was defeated trying to become U.S. Vice President in 1856.
- $ He was again defeated running for U.S. Senate in 1858.

Who could possibly come away from this series of defeats and tragedies and remain optimistic that success was still around the corner? The answer is . . . (drum roll please) . . . **Abraham Lincoln**, elected President of the United States in 1860.

HOW TO BRING MORE JOY AND HAPPINESS INTO YOUR LIFE

Appreciating the beauty of a blossom, the loveliness of a lilac, or the grace of a gazelle are ways in which people can . . . fill their daily lives with . . . pleasure.

—DAVID BUSS, AUTHOR AND PSYCHOLOGIST

As you have probably noticed, I am a huge fan of the groundbreaking work of Dr. Martin Seligman and his positive psychology approach to helping people find lasting joy and happiness in their lives. A more recent book of his, *Authentic Happiness: Using the New Positive Psychology to Realize Your Potential for Lasting Fulfillment* (2002), is packed with self-surveys and practical, well-researched ideas to enrich your life and fulfill your dreams. Armed with insight from the surveys, you can choose specific strategies that Seligman provides for skyrocketing your joy and happiness—permanently!

I strongly recommend reading Seligman's books, but here's a jump start of five Stress Mastery Prescriptions that his research results recommend. You can start working on these today.

℞ № 46

Sustain deep relationships with family and friends, and if possible, maintain a love relationship with a spouse or partner.

℞ № 47

Volunteer and give of yourself to ease the plight of others.

℞ № 48

Practice random acts of kindness on a regular basis (e.g., let a harried mother get in front of you in line or bring Sunday dinner to an elderly couple).

℞ № 49

Maintain close ties to your religion or spiritual foundation, with faith in a good future guiding you. Pray regularly.

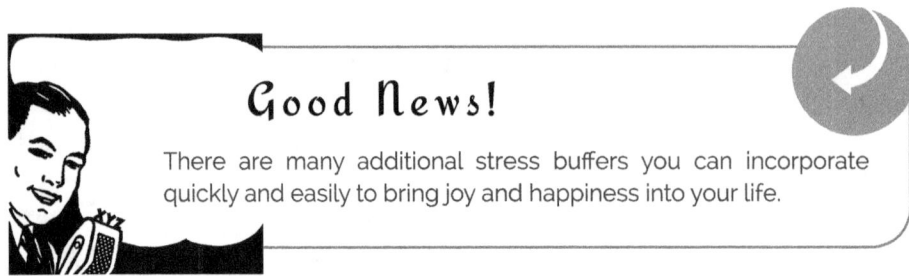

Good News!

There are many additional stress buffers you can incorporate quickly and easily to bring joy and happiness into your life.

Prescription 50 is one that I completed while I was in Denver giving a speech to an audience of professionals. As I was suggesting to my audience that they should pay a gratitude visit to a mentor or someone who has been a special person in their lives, it occurred to me that I had never done that for one of the most important people who ever crossed paths with me. It was Professor Jack Hautaluoma at Colorado State University, just up I-25 from Denver. I made the call, drove up, visited, and he and I both had one of the most emotionally fulfilling experiences of our lives.

℞ № 50

Think of a person in your life who has really meant a lot to you, but to whom you have never fully expressed your appreciation. It could be a former teacher, mentor, co-worker, supervisor, relative, or friend. Take your time composing a letter of appreciation to that person with the details of events that made this person so special to you and have the letter laminated. Then, contact that person and arrange for an in-person visit. Don't tell him or her the purpose of the visit, and be sure to bring the laminated letter as a gift. After visiting, eating, and reminiscing together, take out your letter and read it with emotion and expression. Let the person gather his or her thoughts and respond. You will be amazed at how wonderful both of you will feel.

◆ ◆ ◆

MORE BEHAVIORAL PRESCRIPTIONS TO BUILD RESILIENCY

It's not your aptitude, but your attitude that determines your altitude.
—Zig Ziglar, the late, famous motivational speaker and author

At this point, you have seen 50 Stress Mastery Prescriptions and additional suggestions scattered throughout the chapters. There are certainly many more stress buffers that you can build into your life to help you maintain resiliency in the face of stressful events that will undoubtedly come your way. Make a habit of reviewing the Action Plans at the end of each chapter and following the instructions for keeping on top of your stress and building your resilience.

The 27 behavioral prescriptions listed next have each resulted from rigorous scientific studies in the field of stress prevention and stress mastery. Most are prescriptions you can use in your personal life, but with creativity you can present some to your manager for helping everyone in your work setting to master their stressors.

As you now know, this book actually includes many more than 77 Stress Mastery Prescriptions. Several of the prescriptions have multiple suggestions and there are many more ideas embedded in each chapter. Don't get overwhelmed by the sheer number of these prescriptions and ideas. You certainly don't have to incorporate all of them into your life to be successful. Pick and choose those that work well for you, and perhaps try a few new ones each month. (The entire list of 77 Prescriptions is reproduced in Appendix B for easy reference.)

PROVEN PERSONAL PRESCRIPTIONS

℞ № 51

Connect with people by joining organizations. There are endless examples, from networking to executive coaching clubs, such as Vistage and Mastermind.

℞ № 52

In addition to the relaxation routine described in Appendix C, I have produced a relaxation technique, available on a CD series entitled "Remarkable Resiliency Skills for Uncertain Times" (Singer, 2009). Also, consider taking a yoga class, doing meditation, or even learning self-hypnosis.

You can learn the power of self-hypnosis by visiting with a licensed psychologist who is certified by the American Society of Clinical Hypnosis. I also have available for you a self-hypnosis audio series I produced entitled "Loving the Inner You" (Singer, 2005).

Rx № 53

At bedtime, visualize a very relaxing, pleasurable, serene scene as you drift off to sleep. It could be a real remembrance of a fabulous vacation you took, a childhood memory, or a fantasy place you've dreamed of visiting.

Rx № 54

Treat yourself to a massage at least once a month. Soak in a hot tub or sauna regularly.

Rx № 55

Continue to endeavor to make new, supportive, nonjudgmental friends all through your life.

Rx № 56

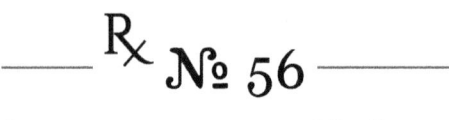

Bring more music into your life. Listening to music and/or playing music releases endorphins, which will calm you. Besides making time to listen to your favorite music, take up an instrument or listen to CDs of the sounds of nature. Listen to your favorite music on the way to and from the office. Sing along in your car and at home. Go to a karaoke bar and sing to your heart's content.

℞ № 57

Make time for satisfying sexual activity in your life. Sexual release is another means of releasing endorphins.

℞ № 58

Start a collection or a hobby. For example, consider cooking, painting, taking a pottery class, or learning a foreign language. Explore the offerings of your local adult education center or college.

℞ № 59

Make a list of things you enjoy doing that are good for you. These can be solo activities or those enjoyed with family members or a significant other. A simple drive out in the country, to a small town, or down by the beach can be very relaxing. Arrange to do at least one each week.

℞ № 60

Frequently explore your senses with activities such as walking barefoot on soft grass, wiggling your toes in mud or wet sand, or riding a bike to feel the wind blowing through your hair.

℞ № 61

Notice color. Research shows that the colors with which you surround yourself directly affect your mood. The three colors that are conducive to relaxation and stress reduction are blue, brown, and pink. Colors to avoid are red, yellow, and green. Use this information in your home decorating, choice of clothes you wear, and even in your office decor.

℞ № 62

Bring a pet into your life.

℞ № 63

Go for rides in the car without a destination in mind. Explore and enjoy peaceful surroundings. Visit picturesque places and bask in the serenity. Go for nostalgic trips to wonderful places from your childhood or visit your old neighborhood.

℞ № 64

Find healthy ways to defuse your frustration or anger on a regular basis. Examples are ballroom dancing, going to the symphony, getting involved in church activities, going to the gym regularly, or screaming to your heart's content at weekend sporting events. I also have available a hypnotic audio program I produced for overcoming anger (Singer, 2012).

Rx № 65

In the face of terrible news beyond your control and beyond healing, find a way to deny what you have been told and pray for improvement. Hope for the best every day, but at the same time, let a tiny piece of you prepare for the worst.

Rx № 66

If you have children, pay attention to the healthy pleasures of parenting. Plan regular, fun, specific activities with your spouse and children. Be sure to put your family at the top of your priority list.

Rx № 67

Be passionate about a mission or purpose in your life and stay focused on it, regardless of detours or roadblocks you run into.

Rx № 68

Live in the now, as opposed to obsessing about past disappointments or worrying about the future. To do this, you must first allow yourself to enjoy the moment and stop rushing through it. So drive slower, select the longest checkout line and the farthest parking space, smile more at people, and stop checking your watch or clock so often.

℞ № 69

Keep a journal or diary of your successes and accomplishments each day, along with listing everything that happened that day for which you are grateful.

℞ № 70

The average person spends a total of about six weeks a year just looking for things! Organize your space and make sure your desk is neat and orderly before you leave the office. Purge your home office of unnecessary clutter. Arrange the things you absolutely need so that you can find them faster, and get rid of everything you're saving for someday reading. Get a lined sheet of paper and print "Things to Do Today" on the top. Make 365 copies so that you can use a new one each day, including both home and office/business reminders. Check each item off after you complete it.

℞ № 71

Be willing to push past your "comfort zone" and try different approaches to prospecting for new clients, dealing with your present clients, etc. Ask yourself how people perceive you and what value you bring to them. Have feedback sessions with high-value clients, soliciting candid feedback about how they perceive you and the value you bring to them. Then focus on that value and bring it to the table whenever you meet with current or prospective clients.

℞ № 72

If you suffer from fear of failure, motivate yourself by recognizing that you will not be able to service clients who really need your expertise if you question yourself and worry. Get over it and start to feel the wonderful feelings associated with knowing you made a real difference in the lives and families of so many clients.

℞ № 73

Encourage your office manager to provide a quiet space, other than the conference room, where advisors can find silence and respite during the workday, or where they can enjoy soft music or relaxation tapes while sitting in a comfortable recliner or reading a paper, etc. Posters of serene scenes can adorn the walls and advisors can mentally escape to those places, even for short breaks in their day. Perhaps refer to this as a "whine and geez" room, where you can complain and feel sorry for yourself all you want.

℞ № 74

If you are new in this career, find an experienced mentor to show you the ropes. Don't feel weak, embarrassed, or incompetent by reaching out to a mentor. Most highly successful advisors begin by having a mentor in their corner, and many continue to have one throughout their careers.

℞ № 75

Reduce your stress by developing two teams: one that will handle busy work—don't try to save money by doing everything yourself (delegate!); and one you can use to cross refer. For example, have a CPA, trust attorney, mergers & acquisitions attorney, and a family law/divorce attorney on your referral team. These will be trusted, competent people to whom you can refer clients and who will also refer clients to you, making the stress of referral generation lighter. You might also consider having college interns on the team to handle the mundane responsibilities at minimal cost to you. Also have other advisors, with whom you have confidence—perhaps from other firms—to refer clients you no longer wish to service.

℞ № 76

Put yourself on a consistent schedule and make a contract with yourself to stick to it, regardless of the temptations to skip things for work. Make sure you get enough sleep, your diet is right, exercise and relaxation activities are included, family time is allocated, etc. If you can't take care of yourself, your success as an advisor will be limited because your body and brain will not sustain the rigors of the job.

℞ № 77

If you have tried to follow these prescriptions but still feel stressed, depressed, anxious, or afraid, talk to a mental-health professional. Choose a PhD- or PsyD-level psychologist who is licensed in your state and who has been practicing for some time. Preferably, look for a professional with a Cognitive Behavior Therapy specialty. Ask your physicians if they have names of professional psychologists with whom their patients have had great outcomes. You can also contact me, since I coach a select group of advisors (1-800-497-9880).

Three years ago Karen had an epiphany and decided to reinvent herself and focus exclusively on women and investing. Aware of the statistic that 70 percent of women fire their financial advisor within the first year of their husbands' deaths, Karen decided to provide women with education that would empower them to take control of their finances. "It was never about the money," Karen said, "but about my deep sense of what I needed to do for my female clients" (personal interview with Karen, 2013).

She also knew the statistics about how many women in the U.S. became widows each year, their net worth, and the projected net worth of widows in the next 20 years. This would be her target population. Furthermore, a major tenet of Karen's plan was to give *every* client the kind of service that used to be available only to high-net-worth clients. Again, she ran into discouragement from primarily male colleagues, but trusted her intuition. Her mantra has always been: "Before I plan, advise, or invest ... I listen to my client."

Karen knew she couldn't succeed in her vision without powerful referral sources, so she collaborated with CPAs and attorneys. She also developed and produced a successful radio show, "Money Sense," which she has now hosted (and funded herself) for more than 20 years and which provides her with a large percentage of referrals each year.

As you can imagine, Karen now runs a very successful firm. It is packed with female advisors, all of whom share her vision and are client hunters, relieving Karen of having the task of the main rainmaker. In the spirit of passing on her passion, one of Karen's advisors is her own daughter, with whom she has now worked for 20 years.

Perhaps as validation for Karen's dream and persistence in overcoming obstacles and naysayers, she has been honored with many awards over the years, including both the "Woman of Influence Award" by the *Milwaukee Business Journal*, and the George Dalton "Inspirational Entrepreneur" Award.

IN CLOSING ... NO ... THIS IS ACTUALLY YOUR BEGINNING!

> *Those who identify with success are welcomed by success; those who identify with failure are likewise welcomed by failure ... the words you choose are the seeds of your future realities.*
>
> —Lao Tzu, Tao Te Ching

Richard Carlson's book title *Don't Sweat the Small Stuff ... and It's All Small Stuff* may sound patronizing and trite, but his message hits home for most of us, including financial advisors.

As Nick Murray (2008) summarizes: "Most financial advisors are ... overworked, underpaid, and chronically stressed out by the seeming randomness of 'performance,' and by the sniping of 'clients' they do not particularly like, and who do not particularly like them" (p. 14).

The kinds of stressors that advisors deal with on a regular basis are unquestionably difficult, but they pale in significance to the stressors our ancestors dealt with as they were forced to hunt down their food and fend off saber-toothed tigers. Yet we turn on the same emergency system inside our brains when we have a difficult client or manager to deal with, and our bodies react as if we are running for our lives. As Robert Sapolsky (1998) concludes in his wonderful book, *Why Zebras Don't Get Ulcers*:

"In our privileged lives, we are uniquely smart enough to have invented these stressors and uniquely foolish enough to have let them, too often, dominate our lives. Surely we have the potential wisdom to banish their stressful hold" (p. 339).

The wisdom that Sapolsky (1998) implores us to use is the same wisdom found in the well-known Serenity Prayer:

God grant me the serenity
To accept the things I cannot change;
Courage to change the things I can;
And wisdom to know the difference.

It is impossible to avoid *all* of life's "slings and arrows" and the worry that comes with them. But you can feel heartened by this old proverb:

> *You cannot prevent the birds of worry and care from flying over your head.*
> *But you can stop them from building a nest in your head.*
> —Unknown

There are endless choices you can make to live a happier, more productive, and healthier life, both at work and in your personal life. You can choose to be a prisoner of your past thinking patterns and continue down that unhappy road. Or, you can choose to take the road less traveled—starting right now. *Today* is the time to begin making significant changes in your life. By doing so, your future becomes your present. The essence of this is captured in Portia Nelson's inspirational, metaphoric poem.

Autobiography in Five Short Chapters

by Portia Nelson

Chapter One

I walk down the street.
There is a deep hole in the sidewalk.
I fall in.
I am lost . . . I am helpless.
It isn't my fault.
It takes forever to find a way out.

Chapter Two

I walk down the street.
There is a deep hole in the sidewalk.
I pretend that I don't see it.
I fall in again.
I can't believe I am in this same place.
But, it isn't my fault.
It still takes a long time to get out.

Chapter Three

I walk down the same street.
There is a deep hole in the sidewalk.
I see it is there.
I still fall in . . . it's a habit . . . but, my eyes are open.
I know where I am.
It is my fault.
I get out immediately.

Chapter Four

I walk down the same street.
There is a deep hole in the sidewalk.
I walk around it.

Chapter Five

I walk down another street.

© 1993 by Portia Nelson, from the book *There's a Hole in My Sidewalk,* Beyond Words Publishing, Hillsboro, OR, pp. 2–3.

So please choose to walk down another street—not by fleeing from your noble profession of safeguarding the wealth that families have entrusted in you—but by identifying and changing the habits that have kept you feeling overwhelmed, stressed, and unhappy. And remember, even if you are not as passionate about your profession as you hoped you'd be at this point in your career, you can still feel passionate about your life. Carol Orsborn (1994), the brilliant author of books based on *I Ching*, the 3,000-year-old work of wisdom, puts it succinctly:

> "Where to begin? Sing in a bathtub. Tap-dance while the computer prints out. Treat yourself to the rarest cheese on the shelf. Take every opportunity to jump out of yourself and into humor, openness, perspective, and faith" (p. 184).

ACTION PLAN FOR STRESS MASTERY

Table 8.4	MY ACTION PLAN FOR STRESS MASTERY

Check each one when you've accomplished it. Feel free to add additional new behaviors in the spaces provided.

New Behavior	What I Did and the Date Accomplished
☐ Every day I will examine negative events in my life and determine whether I am interpreting what happened to me in an optimistic or pessimistic way. ☐ ☐ ☐	What I did: Date accomplished:
☐ I will practice the A-B-C-D-E method of developing optimistic thinking. ☐ ☐ ☐	What I did: Date accomplished:
☐ I will revisit the Thinking-Pattern Worksheet (TPW) and use it to practice the development of optimistic thinking. ☐ ☐ ☐	What I did: Date accomplished:

☐ Twice a month, I will review the list of Stress Mastery Prescriptions in Appendix B and choose one to add to my ongoing practice of building my resilience.	What I did:
☐	
☐	
☐	Date accomplished:

RESOURCES

PREFACE

Cass, A., Lewis, J., & Simco, E. (2000). "Casualties of wall street: an assessment of the walking wounded." Directed Research Study. Fort Lauderdale, Florida: Nova Southeastern University.

Cass, A., Shaw, B., & LeBlanc, S. (2008). *Bullish thinking: The advisor's guide to surviving and thriving on wall street*. New York: Wiley.

Fairchild, C. "Some financial advisors may have PTSD following 2008 crisis: study." Retrieved June 23, 2013, from http://www.huffingtonpost.com/2013/05/11/financial-advisers-ptsd-study_n_3259454.html

Fishel, R. (2003). *Change almost anything in 21 days: Recharge your life with the power of over 500 affirmations*. Deerfield Beach, FL: Health Communications.

Frost, R. (1993). *The road not taken and other poems*. New York: Dover.

Rhode, S. "PTSD caused by money troubles." Retrieved June 23, 2013, from http://www.wral.com/ptsd-caused-by-money-troubles/12033310/

Singer, J.N. (2013). "Do advisors, clients suffer from PTSD?" Retrieved July 17, 2013, from http://www.onwallstreet.com/blogs/advisors-and-ptsd-post-traumatic-stress-2685812-1.html

CHAPTER ONE

American Institute of Stress. (n.d.) "America's number one health problem." Retrieved April 10, 2009, from http://www.stress.org/Americas.htm

American Psychological Association. (2007, October 24). "Stress is a major health problem in the U.S., warns APA." Retrieved April 10, 2009, from http://www.apa.org/releases/stressproblem.html

American Psychological Association. (2008, October 7). "APA poll finds women bear brunt of nation's stress, financial downturn." Retrieved April 10, 2009, from http://www.apa.org/releases/women-stress1008.html

Cass, A., Lewis, J., & Simco, E. (2000). "Casualties of wall street: an assessment of the walking wounded." Directed Research Study. Fort Lauderdale, Florida: Nova Southeastern University.

Cass, A., Shaw, B., & LeBlanc, S. (2008). *Bullish thinking: The advisor's guide to surviving and thriving on wall street.* New York: Wiley.

Charlesworth, E. A., & Nathan, R. A. (1984). *Stress management: A comprehensive guide to wellness.* New York: Ballantine Books.

Goleman, D., & Gurin, J. (Eds.) (1993). *Mind body medicine.* Yonkers, NY: Consumer Report Books.

Helpguide.org. (n.d.) "Understanding stress." Retrieved June 4, 2009, from http://www.helpguide.org/mental/stress_signs.htm

Sapolsky, R. (1998). *Why zebras don't get ulcers.* New York: Freeman.

Seligman, M. E. (1998). *Learned optimism.* New York: Pocket Books.

Seyle, H. (1976). *The stress of life.* New York: Ballantine Books.

CHAPTER TWO

Atkinson, W. (2004). *Eliminate stress from your life forever.* New York: Amacom.

Culligan, M. J., & Sedlacek, J. and K. (1988). *How to avoid stress before it kills you.* New York: Random House.

Hawkins, N. G., Davies, R., & Holmes, T. H. (1957). "Evidence of psychosocial factors in the development of pulmonary tuberculosis." *American Review of Tuberculosis and Pulmonary Diseases, 75,* 768–780.

Holmes, T. H., & Masuda, M. (1970). "Life change and illness susceptibility." Paper presented at the annual meeting of the American Association for the Advancement of Science, Chicago, IL.

Holmes, T. H., & Rahe, R. H. (1967a). "Schedule of recent experiences." Seattle: University of Washington School of Medicine.

Holmes, T. H., & Rahe, R. H. (1967b). "The social readjustment rating scale." *Journal of Psychosomatic Research, 11,* 213–218.

Miller, M., & Rahe, R. H. (1997). "Life changing scaling for the 1990s." *Journal of Psychosomatic Research, 43,* 279–292.

Seyle, H. (1976). *The stress of life.* New York: Ballantine Books.

CHAPTER THREE

Burns, D. (1989). *The feeling good handbook.* New York: William Morrow.

Clance, P.R. (1985). *Impostor phenomenon.* Atlanta: Peachtree Publishers.

Helmstetter, S. (1987). *The self-talk solution.* New York: Pocket Books.

Helmstetter, S. (1982). *What to say when you talk to yourself.* New York: Pocket Books.

James, William. (n.d.). Quote. ThinkExist.com. Retrieved September 29, 2009, from http://thinkexist.com/quotation/the_greatest_weapon_against_stress_is_our_ability/330010.html

McKay, M. D. (1981). *Thoughts & feelings.* Oakland, CA: New Harbinger.

Pulos, L. (March 2004). "Sports psychology and performance enhancement." Paper Presented at a meeting of the American Society of Clinical Hypnosis, Denver, CO.

Seyle, H. (1976). *The stress of life.* New York: Ballantine Books.

Singer, J. N. (1995). "Conquering your internal critic so you can sing your own song." In D. M. Walters (Ed.), *Great speakers anthology* (Vol. 4, pp. 160–195). Glendora, CA: Royal.

Singer, J. N. (2013). "Advisors: Recognize distorted thinking habits." Retrieved July 25, 2013, from http://www.onwallstreet.com/blogs/avoiding-fear-on-the-way-to-success-2685387-1.html

Singer, J. N. (2013). "Creating a game plan for success to conquer self-doubt." Retrieved July 10, 2013, from http://www.onwallstreet.com/blogs/creating-a-game-plan-for-success-2685724-1.html

Singer, J. N. (2013). "Four steps to reduce stress." Retrieved August 27, 2013, from http://www.onwallstreet.com/blogs/advisors-steps-to-reduce- stress-2686391-1.html

Singer, J. N. (2013). "How advisors can avoid fear of failure." Retrieved June 18, 2013, from http://www.onwallstreet.com/blogs/avoiding-fear-on-the-way-to-success-2685387-1.html

Singer, J. N. (2013). "Solutions for the stress of wealth management." Retrieved August 7, 2013, from http://www.onwallstreet.com/blogs/advisors-learn-how-to-manage-stress-2686137-1.html

Singer, J. N. (2013). "What advisors can learn from Joe Flacco." Retrieved January 3, 2014, from http://www.producersweb.com/r/pwebmc/d/contentFocus/?pcID=8f75fd3c5026abe5f5a2ccf356646f46

CHAPTER FOUR

American Institute of Stress. (n.d.). "America's number one health problem." Retrieved April 10, 2009, from http://www.stress.org/Americas.htm

Braiker, H. B. (1995). *The disease to please.* New York: McGraw-Hill.

Bristol, C. M., & Sherman, H. (1987). *TNT: The power within you.* New York: Prentice Hall.

Cass, A., Shaw, B. F., & LeBlanc, S. (2008). *Bullish thinking.* Hoboken, N.J.: Wiley.

Dudley, G.W., & Goodson, S. L. (2007). *The psychology of sales call reluctance.* Dallas: Behavioral Sciences Research Press.

Fensterheim, H., & Baer, J. (1975). *Don't say "yes" when you want to say "no."* New York: Dell.

Friedman, M., & Rosenman, R. H. (1974). *Type-A behavior and your heart.* New York: Knopf.

Friedman, M., & Ulmer, D. (1984). *Treating type-A behavior and your heart.* New York: Fawcett.

Helmstetter, S. (1982). *What to say when you talk to yourself.* New York: Pocket Books.

Lakein, A. (1973). *How to get control of your time and your life.* New York: NewAmerican Library.

McKay, M., & Davis, M. (1981). *Thoughts & feelings.* Oakland, CA: New Harbinger.

McKay, M., & Rogers, P. (1985). *The anger control workbook.* Oakland, CA: New Harbinger.

Roskies, E. (1987). *Stress management for the healthy type-A.* New York: Guilford.

Sapolsky, R. (1998). *Why zebras don't get ulcers.* New York: Freeman.

Seyle, H. (1976). *The stress of life.* New York: Ballantine Books.

Singer, J. (2009). *Mastering anger management.* Dallas, TX: Hypnosis Network.

CHAPTER FIVE

Beck, A. T., & Emory, G. (1986). *Anxiety disorders and phobias.* New York: Basic Books.

Clance, P. R. (1985). *Impostor phenomenon.* Atlanta: Peachtree Publishers.

Mahoney, M. J. (1971). "The self-management of covert behavior: A case study." *Behavior Therapy, 2,* 575–578.

McKay, M., & Davis, M. (1981). *Thoughts & feelings.* Oakland, CA: New Harbinger.

Seyle, H. (1976). *The stress of life.* New York: Ballantine Books.

Shelton, J. L., & Levy, R. L. (1981). *Behavioral assignments and treatment compliance.* Champaign, IL: Research Press.

Singer, J. (2006). Interview with Dr. Jack Singer. In D. Wright (Ed.), *Dynamic health* (pp. 1–15). Sevierville, TN: Insight.

Singer, J. N. (1995). "Conquering your internal critic so you can sing your own song." In D. M. Walters (Ed.), *Great speakers anthology,* (Vol. 4, pp. 160–195). Glendora, CA: Royal.

CHAPTER SIX

Bandura, A. (1994). "Self-efficacy." In V.S. Ramachaudran (Ed.), *Encyclopedia of human behavior* (Vol. 4, pp. 71–81). New York: Academic Press. (Reprinted in H. Friedman [Ed.], *Encyclopedia of mental health*. San Diego: Academic Press, 1998).

Bristol, C. M., & Sherman, H. (1997). *TNT: The power within you.* New York: Prentice Hall.

Burns, D. (1989). *The feeling good handbook.* New York: William Morrow.

Fishel, R. (2003). *Change almost anything in 21 days: Recharge your life with the power of over 500 affirmations.* Deerfield Beach, FL: Health Communications.

Helmstetter, S. (1987). *The self-talk solution.* New York: Pocket Books.

Maddi, S. R. (2002). "The story of hardiness: Twenty years of theorizing, research, and practice." *Consulting Psychology Journal, 54,* 173–185.

Maddi, S. R. (2006). "Hardiness: The courage to be resilient." In J. C. Thomas, D. L. Segal, & M. Herson (Eds.), *Comprehensive handbook of personality and psychopathology: Personality and everyday functioning.* (Vol.1, pp. 306–321). Hoboken, NJ: Wiley.

Maddi, S. R. (2008). "The courage and strategies of hardiness as helpful in growing despite major, disruptive stresses." *American Psychologist, 63*(6), 563–564.

Maddi, S. R., & Khoshaba, D. M. (2005). *Resilience at work.* New York: Amacom.

Khoshaba, D. M., & Maddi, S. R. (1999). *Hardiness training: Managing stressful change.* Newport Beach, CA: Hardiness Institute.

Pulos, L. (March 2004). "Sports psychology and performance enhancement." Paper presented at a meeting of the American Society of Clinical Hypnosis, Denver, CO.

Singer, J. N. (1974). "Participative decision-making about work: An overdue look at variables which mediate its effects." *Sociology of Work and Occupations, 1*(4), 347–371.

CHAPTER SEVEN

Allianz Life. "The 2013 Allianz women, money and power study." Retrieved September 29, 2013, from https://www.allianzlife.com/Variable/content/public/Literature/Documents/ENT-1462-N.pd

Blumenthal, B. "8 toxic personalities to avoid." Retrieved July 21, 2013, from http://shine.yahoo.com/work-money/8-toxic-personalities-to-avoid-461078.html

Britt, S. "Researcher finds correlation between financial arguments, decreased relationship satisfaction." Retrieved September 28, 2013, from http://www.k-state.edu/media/newsreleases/jul13/predictingdivorce71113.html

Buchanan, H. (2011). *Selling financial services to women.* Richmond, VA: Hachette.

Cass, A., Shaw, B. F., & LeBlanc, S. (2008). *Bullish thinking.* Hoboken, N.J.: Wiley.

Cass, A., Shaw, R. F., & LeBlanc, S. (2008). *The bullish thinking guide for managers.* Hoboken, N.J.: Wiley.

Fidelity Investments. "Couples retirement study." Retrieved September 2, 2013, from https://www.fidelity.com/viewpoints/personal-finance/couples-and-finances.

Fidelity Investments (2013a). "Fidelity provides information and tools that help advisors design action plans to deepen relationships with female clients." Retrieved September 2, 2013, from www.fidelity/using-an-advisor/fidelity-provides-information-and-tools-that-help-advisors-engage-female-clients

Glass, L. (1995). *Toxic people.* New York: St. Martin's Griffin.

Heckman, A. M. "Advisors: How to know when your female clients are happy." Retrieved November 5, 2013, from http://www.adrimillerheckman.com/your-pink-office/financial-advisors-how-to-know-when-your-female-clients-are-happy/

Kingsbury, K. B. (2013). *How to give financial advice to women.* New York: McGraw-Hill.

Miller, M., & Buchanan, H. (2010). *The soccer mom myth.* Austin, TX: Wizard Academy Press.

Murray, N. (2008). *Behavioral investment counseling.* New York: The Nick Murray Company, Inc.

Murray, N. (1999). *The craft of advice.* New York: The Nick Murray Company, Inc.

Singer, J. (2013). "Communications skills for advisors." Retrieved November 24, 2013, from http://tinyurl.com/communications-skills

Singer, J. N. (2013). "Capitalizing on the female market." Retrieved November 25, 2013, from http://www.onwallstreet.com/blogs/capitalizing-on-the-female-market-2687399-1.html

Singer, J. N. (2013). "The psychology of money: How to help your clients change their beliefs." Retrieved January 3, 2014, from http://www.producersweb.com/r/pwebmc/d/contentFocus/?pcID=5f531b0cd4118a04f09c33d596ef11d2

Singer, J. N. (2013). "Understanding the female market." Retrieved October 27, 2013, from http://www.onwallstreet.com/blogs/understanding-the-female-mdarket-2687075-1.html

Sofia, R., Fross, T., Fross, R., & Rollins, C. (2011). Members Only. The Villages, FL: Platinum Advisor Marketing Strategies.

Wojnar, K., & Meek, C. "Women's views of wealth and the planning process: It's their values that matter, not just their value." Retrieved June 23, 2013, from http://tinyurl.com/wealth-and-planning

CHAPTER EIGHT

Bristol, C. M., & Sherman, H. (1987). *TNT: The power within you.* New York: Simon & Schuster.

Carlson, R. (1997). *Don't sweat the small stuff . . . and it's all small stuff.* New York: Hyperion.

Frost, R. (1993). *The road not taken and other poems.* New York: Dover.

Haven, B. Q., Frandsen, K. J., Karren, & Hooker, K. R. (1992). *The health effects of attitudes, emotions, relationships.* Provo, UT: EMS Associates.

Murray, N. (2008). *Behavioral investment counseling.* New York: The Nick Murray Company, Inc.

Nelson, P. (1993). *There's a hole in my sidewalk.* Hillsboro, OR: Beyond Words.

Orsborn, C. (1994). *How would confucius ask for a raise?* New York: Morrow.

Peterson, C., & Bossio, L. M. (1993). "Healthy attitudes: Optimism, hope, and control." In D. Goleman & J. Gurin (Eds.), *Mind body medicine: How to use your mind for better health* (pp. 351–366). Yonkers, NY: Consumer Reports Books.

Sapolsky, R. (1998). *Why zebras don't get ulcers.* New York: Freeman.

Seligman, M. E. (1998). *Learned Optimism.* New York: Pocket Books.

Seligman, M. E. (2002). *Authentic happiness: Using the new positive psychology to realize your potential for lasting fulfillment.* New York: The Free Press.

Siegel, B. S. (1986). *Love, medicine & miracles.* New York: HarperCollins.

Siegel, B. S. (1998). *Peace, love & healing.* New York: Harper & Row.

Singer, J. (2001). *How to permanently master your anger.* Laguna Niguel, CA: Psychologically Speaking, with Dr. Jack Singer, LLC.

Singer, J. (2005). *Loving the inner you!* Laguna Niguel, CA: Psychologically Speaking, with Dr. Jack Singer, LLC.

Singer, J. (2009). *Remarkable resiliency skills for uncertain times.* Laguna Niguel, CA: Psychologically Speaking, with Dr. Jack Singer, LLC.

Singer, J.N. (2013). "Your game plan for releasing your inner champion in your business." Retrieved April 24, 2013, from http://www.producersweb.com/r/pwebmc/d/contentFocus/?pcID=63105f7bdbca78e428798766447a6865

Sobel, D. S., & Ornstein, R. (1996). *The healthy mind healthy body handbook.* New York: Patient Education Media.

APPENDIX A

GLOSSARY *of* ACRONYMS

CHAPTERS 1, 4, AND 5

SNS (sympathetic nervous system):

This is frequently referred to as the fight-or-flight nervous system. The SNS switches on whenever people sense danger, but it also switches on whenever people even think about something that worries or bothers them. Once the SNS is activated, the body goes into emergency mode, and this leads to a spike in strain symptoms, including muscle tightening and blood pressure elevation. Because we can learn to control our thinking, we can ultimately learn the trigger-thought patterns that we habitually use, which ultimately switch on the SNS and cause our strain. Once we understand those patterns, we can learn how to avoid triggering the SNS.

CHAPTER 2

LCUs (life-change units):

These point totals attribute to each event on the RLCQ. The more LCUs one accumulates in a 12-month period, the greater the probability of stress-related illness or emotional difficulties befalling that person in the next 12 months.

RLCQ (Recent Life Changes Questionnaire):

This is a researched-based, 70-event questionnaire that helps you determine how many stress points you have accumulated because of the changes you have made in the last 12 months. The more points you have, the greater probability that you are suffering from stress-related symptoms. Keeping track of your stress points over any 12-month period helps you make important decisions to modify the changes you make in your life during the next 12 months.

CHAPTER 4

CHD (coronary heart disease):
Cited by the American Medical Association as the most important modern health problem in the United States, where each year more than half a million Americans die from coronary heart disease (Roskies, 1987).

CHAPTERS 5 AND 8

A->B->C->D->E model:
This is an easy way to understand the process of stress provocations and how to avoid stress outcomes. **A**ctivating events lead to internal **B**eliefs and thoughts about those events, which leads to the **C**onsequent emotions and behaviors, which can then be modified by engaging **D**isputing thoughts, leading to **E**nergized, healthy, revitalized emotions.

TPW (Thinking-Pattern Worksheet):
This chart organizes your thoughts, the self-defeating thinking pattern you habitually use, and the disputing thoughts that will eliminate or prevent stress outcomes.

CHAPTER 6

The Three Cs of Hardiness (Commitment, Control, and Challenge):
These are the primary determinants of psychological hardiness or stress resistance. Once you learn to develop or increase these traits in your own life, you will make a giant leap toward ultimately buffering yourself from the impact of stress.

REFERENCE

Roskies, E. (1987). *Stress management for the healthy type-A*. New York: Guilford Press.

APPENDIX B

77 BEHAVIORAL PRESCRIPTIONS *to* MASTER STRESS *and* BUILD YOUR RESILIENCE

 ### STRESS MASTERY PRESCRIPTION #1

Take care of your emotional health by taking care of your physical health. Consider visiting a licensed naturopathic physician to learn about foods and natural supplements that have been proven to reduce and prevent stress. The following are examples of healthy habits that have been shown to directly impact moods and stress levels:

- *Keep your blood sugar low with frequent, smaller meals that include protein.*
- *Eat light at night.*
- *Get ample sleep.*
- *Avoid alcohol, caffeine, and tobacco.*
- *Load up on antioxidant-rich foods.*
- *Keep your weight in the normal range for your age and height.*

 ### STRESS MASTERY PRESCRIPTION #2

Practice breathing through your diaphragm. Put your hands on your stomach and breathe deeply in through your nose and exhale through your mouth, so that your hands move out when you inhale and move back in when you exhale. If your hands are not moving and only your shoulders and chest move when you breathe deeply, you are engaging in shallow, less relaxing breathing. You can easily teach yourself to breathe through your diaphragm with practice.

Stress Mastery Prescription #3

Recognize that you can live with a certain amount of stress in your life and that it may even be beneficial to you.

Stress Mastery Prescription #4

Ask yourself what calm people do to maintain their stress levels. Examples of answers to that question are jogging or walking each morning before work, making time for lunch each day with a calm friend or colleague, and reading articles or the rest of this book on how to master the stresses in life.

Stress Mastery Prescription #5

Stay fit. Run, bike, swim, walk, or hike each week. Aerobic (heart rate increasing) exercise releases endorphins—chemicals that reduce stress. Other ways to benefit from exercise are dancing, gardening, or raking leaves. You don't have to engage in vigorous activity to benefit.

Stress Mastery Prescription #6

If you have had too much change on your plate in the last year, delay new changes that you can control for at least six months, such as tackling an evening course directed at attaining your MBA. Simply delay the course for several months and then engage in it.

Stress Mastery Prescription #7

Let go of resentment you are holding toward anyone or anything. Don't harbor grudges. Forgive those who have hurt you and move on.

Stress Mastery Prescription #8

For the next two weeks, keep a pad next to your bed. Each night, reflect on the day's activities and events. Write, on separate lines, at least five things you are grateful for that occurred during the last 24 hours.

Stress Mastery Prescription #9

Recognize that you are not a prisoner of past programming. Just because you heard negative comments from your parents and others does not make those statements accurate. You can choose to disregard them, and you can decide not to repeat them to yourself. Instead, repeat healthy, optimistic thoughts to yourself daily.

STRESS MASTERY PRESCRIPTION #10

The next time you feel any negative emotion (overwhelm, depression, irritation, impatience, or hopelessness), list the specific thoughts that went through your mind just before you felt that emotion. This is the first step in recovering from your stress.

 STRESS MASTERY PRESCRIPTION #11

Recognize the specific negative self-talk patterns you have developed. Make a list of typical negative thoughts you have in an average day and check the list of 10 common distorted-thinking patterns to determine which ones you engage in regularly.

 STRESS MASTERY PRESCRIPTION #12

Whenever you recognize that you are upset and thinking negatively, use the quick reference guide of questions to challenge that negative thinking.

 STRESS MASTERY PRESCRIPTION #13

Review Table 4.1, Checklist of Potential Type-A Behaviors, to see if you fit this profile.

 STRESS MASTERY PRESCRIPTION #14

Simplify your life. Ask yourself what really needs to be done. If you don't perform a specific task right now, what's the worst that will happen? Get a good spam blocker so you can avoid having to read the bulk of your e-mails, and be selective regarding the number of people to whom you give your e-mail address. Read Lakein's How to Get Control of Your Time and Your Life *(1973).*

 STRESS MASTERY PRESCRIPTION #15

Learn to be flexible and just go with the flow. As the Quaker proverb goes: "In the face of strong winds, let me be a blade of grass. In the face of strong walls, let me be a gale of wind" (Sapolsky, 1998, p. 416).

 STRESS MASTERY PRESCRIPTION #16

The next time you feel any negative emotion, revisit Table 4.1 to see if you are engaging in these behaviors. Then, use the information in this chapter to modify these behaviors.

Stress Mastery Prescription #17

Become aware of the triggers to your stress feelings.

Stress Mastery Prescription #18

Find a relaxation technique you're comfortable with and make it part of your daily routine. See Appendix C for a relaxation example. Practice your relaxation skills in a place where you will be left alone and not interrupted by the phone, TV, or other people.

Stress Mastery Prescription #19

Use short relaxation exercises several times a day.

Stress Mastery Prescription #20

Get in touch with your false beliefs and change them.

Stress Mastery Prescription #21

Recognize the price you are paying to achieve more and more in less and less time.

Stress Mastery Prescription #22

Get a time-management book, and practice the techniques you learn from it.

Stress Mastery Prescription #23

Never skip or shorten breakfast.

Stress Mastery Prescription #24

Take multiple mini-breaks during the day.

Stress Mastery Prescription #25

Break up your work routine by taking the time to go for a walk, meditate, or listen to soothing music or your relaxation routine on your iPod, smart phone, iPad, or portable CD player.

APPENDIX B | 77 BEHAVIORAL PRESCRIPTIONS

STRESS MASTERY PRESCRIPTION #26

Make a deal with yourself that you will never leave the office later than 6:00 p.m. (unless you have a meeting scheduled).

STRESS MASTERY PRESCRIPTION #27

Each day, make a deal with yourself to accomplish one task at a time, rather than overwhelming yourself with multiple tasks.

STRESS MASTERY PRESCRIPTION #28

Pay attention to your angry and hostile behaviors, and learn to modify them using anger-mastery techniques.

STRESS MASTERY PRESCRIPTION #29

Practice active-listening techniques. Take a course in Active Listening. Begin practicing this technique at home, and once you are comfortable with it, use it with your clients.

STRESS MASTERY PRESCRIPTION #30

Review the people-pleasing behaviors in Table 4.2 to see if you fit this profile.

STRESS MASTERY PRESCRIPTION #31

Learn how to assert yourself without feeling guilty.

STRESS MASTERY PRESCRIPTION #32

To help you recognize your assertiveness choices, use the form in Table 4.9 and describe each situation where you had a choice but behaved nonassertively.

STRESS MASTERY PRESCRIPTION #33

Take notice and keep a record of situations in which you were assertive, and reward yourself accordingly.

Stress Mastery Prescription #34

Catch yourself whenever you are awfulizing and stop it immediately, using the TPW (Table 5.1) on page 106.

Stress Mastery Prescription #35

The next time you feel any negative emotion (e.g., overwhelm, fright, depression, irritation, impatience, hopelessness), do the following: Use the TPW and describe the event that led to the emotions; write down the specific emotions you feel and rate them. Write down the automatic thoughts that preceded your feeling those emotions, and determine which distortion patterns those thoughts fit. Then write down rebuttal thoughts that make sense. Believing those rebuttal thoughts should help you feel better.

Stress Mastery Prescription #36

When you don't have time to use the TPW, use the thought-stopping, calming-breathing, write-it-down, or worry-time techniques described next.

Stress Mastery Prescription #37

Don't try to control that which cannot be controlled or things that have already happened. Stick with what you are capable of controlling in the present.

Stress Mastery Prescription #38

Make a list of your short- and long-term goals, right now, and answer the eight questions listed in Table 6.3 for each goal.

Stress Mastery Prescription #39

To develop attitudes of hardiness, and to stick to your goals, start using positive affirmations daily. Write down or record your affirmations and read or listen to them at least 10 times a day for a minimum of 21 days.

Stress Mastery Prescription #40

Understand the basic personality traits of toxic people. If you see these traits in your clients and they are causing you stress, eliminate them from your practice.

STRESS MASTERY PRESCRIPTION #41

Avoid negative people, and if you cannot avoid them altogether, let their negative messages and feedback about you go in one ear and out the other. Notice the good things you love about the people in your life, and ignore the things you don't love about them. Make sure there are happy, fun-loving people in your life, and stay away from bitter, disgruntled people.

 STRESS MASTERY PRESCRIPTION #42

Understand your core values regarding investment and wealth management/enhancement strategies for your clients and stick to them, despite temptations to compromise them in order to please a client.

 STRESS MASTERY PRESCRIPTION #43

Build into your prospecting plan the goal of soliciting more female clients, and be proactive in dealing with the female (and spouses of male) clients you have currently. Have meetings with female spouses <u>alone</u>, in order to understand their unique concerns. Make it safe for them to discuss issues, which they may not relate to you in a joint meeting with their spouse.

 STRESS MASTERY PRESCRIPTION #44

Review the suggestions for attracting female clients to your practice and accommodating their needs, fears, and goals. Then practice the active listening skills you are working on with all prospective and active clients, especially female.

 STRESS MASTERY PRESCRIPTION #45

Using the TPWs in Tables 8.2 and 8.3, practice interpreting unfortunate events in optimistic ways.

 STRESS MASTERY PRESCRIPTION #46

Sustain deep relationships with family and friends, and if possible, maintain a love relationship with a spouse or partner.

 STRESS MASTERY PRESCRIPTION #47

Volunteer and give of yourself to ease the plight of others.

Stress Mastery Prescription #48

Practice random acts of kindness on a regular basis (e.g., let a harried mother get in front of you in line or bring Sunday dinner to an elderly couple).

Stress Mastery Prescription #49

Maintain close ties to your religion or spiritual foundation, with faith in a good future guiding you. Pray regularly.

Stress Mastery Prescription #50

Think of a person in your life who has really meant a lot to you, but to whom you have never fully expressed your appreciation. It could be a former teacher, mentor, co-worker, supervisor, relative, or friend. Take your time composing a letter of appreciation to that person with the details of events that made this person so special to you and have the letter laminated. Then, contact that person and arrange for an in-person visit. Don't tell him or her the purpose of the visit, and be sure to bring the laminated letter as a gift. After visiting, eating, and reminiscing together, take out your letter and read it with emotion and expression. Let the person gather his or her thoughts and respond. You will be amazed at how wonderful both of you will feel.

Stress Mastery Prescription #51

Connect with people by joining organizations. There are endless examples, from networking to executive coaching clubs, such as Vistage and Mastermind.

Stress Mastery Prescription #52

In addition to the relaxation routine described in Appendix C, I have produced a relaxation technique, available on a CD series entitled "Remarkable Resiliency Skills for Uncertain Times" (Singer, 2009). Also, consider taking a yoga class, doing meditation, or even learning self-hypnosis. You can learn the power of self-hypnosis by visiting with a licensed psychologist who is certified by the American Society of Clinical Hypnosis. I also have available for you a self-hypnosis audio series I produced entitled "Loving the Inner You" (Singer, 2005).

Stress Mastery Prescription #53

At bedtime, visualize a very relaxing, pleasurable, serene scene as you drift off to sleep. It could be a real remembrance of a fabulous vacation you took, a childhood memory, or a fantasy place you've dreamed of visiting.

Stress Mastery Prescription #54

Treat yourself to a massage at least once a month. Soak in a hot tub or sauna regularly.

Stress Mastery Prescription #55

Continue to endeavor to make new, supportive, nonjudgmental friends all through your life.

Stress Mastery Prescription #56

Bring more music into your life. Listening to music and/or playing music releases endorphins, which will calm you. Besides making time to listen to your favorite music, take up an instrument or listen to CDs of the sounds of nature. Listen to your favorite music on the way to and from the office. Sing along in your car and at home. Go to a karaoke bar and sing to your heart's content.

Stress Mastery Prescription #57

Make time for satisfying sexual activity in your life. Sexual release is another means of releasing endorphins.

Stress Mastery Prescription #58

Start a collection or a hobby. For example, consider cooking, painting, taking a pottery class, or learning a foreign language. Explore the offerings of your local adult education center or college.

Stress Mastery Prescription #59

Make a list of things you enjoy doing that are good for you. These can be solo activities or those enjoyed with family members or a significant other. A simple drive out in the country, to a small town, or down by the beach can be very relaxing. Arrange to do at least one each week.

Stress Mastery Prescription #60

Frequently explore your senses with activities such as walking barefoot on soft grass, wiggling your toes in mud or wet sand, or riding a bike to feel the wind blowing through your hair.

Stress Mastery Prescription #61

Notice color. Research shows that the colors with which you surround yourself directly affect your mood. The three colors that are conducive to relaxation and stress reduction are blue, brown, and pink. Colors to avoid are red, yellow, and green. Use this information in your home decorating, choice of clothes you wear, and even in your office decor.

Stress Mastery Prescription #62

Bring a pet into your life.

Stress Mastery Prescription #63

Go for rides in the car without a destination in mind. Explore and enjoy peaceful surroundings. Visit picturesque places and bask in the serenity. Go for nostalgic trips to wonderful places from your childhood or visit your old neighborhood.

Stress Mastery Prescription #64

Find healthy ways to defuse your frustration or anger on a regular basis. Examples are ballroom dancing, going to the symphony, getting involved in church activities, going to the gym regularly, or screaming to your heart's content at weekend sporting events. I also have available a hypnotic audio program I produced for overcoming anger (Singer, 2012).

Stress Mastery Prescription #65

In the face of terrible news beyond your control and beyond healing, find a way to deny what you have been told and pray for improvement. Hope for the best every day, but at the same time, let a tiny piece of you prepare for the worst.

Stress Mastery Prescription #66

If you have children, pay attention to the healthy pleasures of parenting. Plan regular, fun, specific activities with your spouse and children. Be sure to put your family at the top of your priority list.

Stress Mastery Prescription #67

Be passionate about a mission or purpose in your life and stay focused on it, regardless of detours or roadblocks you run into.

STRESS MASTERY PRESCRIPTION #68

Live in the now, as opposed to obsessing about past disappointments or worrying about the future. To do this, you must first allow yourself to enjoy the moment and stop rushing through it. So drive slower, select the longest checkout line and the farthest parking space, smile more at people, and stop checking your watch or clock so often.

 STRESS MASTERY PRESCRIPTION #69

Keep a journal or diary of your successes and accomplishments each day, along with listing everything that happened that day for which you are grateful.

 STRESS MASTERY PRESCRIPTION #70

The average person spends a total of about six weeks a year just looking for things! Organize your space and make sure your desk is neat and orderly before you leave the office. Purge your home office of unnecessary clutter. Arrange the things you absolutely need so that you can find them faster, and get rid of everything you're saving for someday reading. Get a lined sheet of paper and print "Things to Do Today" on the top. Make 365 copies so that you can use a new one each day, including both home and office/business reminders. Check each item off after you complete it.

 STRESS MASTERY PRESCRIPTION #71

Be willing to push past your "comfort zone" and try different approaches to prospecting for new clients, dealing with your present clients, etc. Ask yourself how people perceive you and what value you bring to them. Have feedback sessions with high-value clients, soliciting candid feedback about how they perceive you and the value you bring to them. Then focus on that value and bring it to the table whenever you meet with current or prospective clients.

 STRESS MASTERY PRESCRIPTION #72

If you suffer from fear of failure, motivate yourself by recognizing that you will not be able to service clients who really need your expertise if you question yourself and worry. Get over it and start to feel the wonderful feelings associated with knowing you made a real difference in the lives and families of so many clients.

STRESS MASTERY PRESCRIPTION #73

Encourage your office manager to provide a quiet space, other than the conference room, where advisors can find silence and respite during the workday, or where they can enjoy soft music or relaxation tapes while sitting in a comfortable recliner or reading a paper, etc. Posters of serene scenes can adorn the walls and advisors can mentally escape to those places, even for short breaks in their day. Perhaps refer to this as a "whine and geez" room, where you can complain and feel sorry for yourself all you want.

 STRESS MASTERY PRESCRIPTION #74

If you are new in this career, find an experienced mentor to show you the ropes. Don't feel weak, embarrassed, or incompetent by reaching out to a mentor. Most highly successful advisors begin by having a mentor in their corner, and many continue to have one throughout their careers.

 STRESS MASTERY PRESCRIPTION #75

Reduce your stress by developing two teams: one that will handle busy work—don't try to save money by doing everything yourself (delegate!); and one you can use to cross refer. For example, have a CPA, trust attorney, mergers & acquisitions attorney, and a family law/divorce attorney on your referral team. These will be trusted, competent people to whom you can refer clients and who will also refer clients to you, making the stress of referral generation lighter. You might also consider having college interns on the team to handle the mundane responsibilities at minimal cost to you. Also have other advisors, with whom you have confidence—perhaps from other firms—to refer clients you no longer wish to service.

 STRESS MASTERY PRESCRIPTION #76

Put yourself on a consistent schedule and make a contract with yourself to stick to it, regardless of the temptations to skip things for work. Make sure you get enough sleep, your diet is right, exercise and relaxation activities are included, family time is allocated, etc. If you can't take care of yourself, your success as an advisor will be limited because your body and brain will not sustain the rigors of the job.

 STRESS MASTERY PRESCRIPTION #77

If you have tried to follow these prescriptions but still feel stressed, depressed, anxious, or afraid, talk to a mental-health professional. Choose a PhD- or PsyD-level psychologist who is licensed in your state and who has been practicing for some time. Preferably, look for a professional with a Cognitive Behavior Therapy specialty. Ask your physicians if they have names of professional psychologists with whom their patients have had great outcomes. You can also contact me, since I coach a select group of advisors (1-800-497-9880).

APPENDIX C

A DEEP-MUSCLE RELAXATION TECHNIQUE

Place yourself on your most relaxing chair, bed, or couch, making sure that your neck is supported when your head rests back comfortably. Make sure you will not be disturbed or interrupted for the next 15 minutes or so. Turn your phones, TVs, and radios off. When you listen to this recording, be in a place where your attention will <u>not</u> be required, such as while driving a car.

Now, read this script into a recorder slowly, in a very calm and monotone voice. Either use your own voice or ask someone whose voice is soothing and calming to record it for you. You can use a digital recorder, from which you can either burn a CD from the recording or download it directly to your iPod, iPhone, or other MP3 device like you do with music. When recording this script, go slowly and pause wherever you see the dots (. . .).

(BEGIN RECORDING HERE)

I am getting in a very comfortable position . . . a position that is going to be perfect for me with no distractions, no phones ringing, and no people trying to get my attention . . .

I will block everything out of my mind that might get in the way of focusing my concentration completely and totally on the task at hand . . . I will give myself an opportunity to get into a very relaxed state, which will raise my overall level of peacefulness and calm . . . I can even give myself some suggestions to remain calm, even under the most trying circumstances in my job.

For example, professional singers and musicians have learned that the most powerful form of breathing during their performances is through their diaphragms. That method not only brings in more oxygen, but also quickly relieves excess tension. Now, I can learn to do the same thing . . . easily. The way I'll know when I am truly breathing through my diaphragm is that when I inhale deeply through my nose, my stomach pushes out, and when I exhale through my mouth, my stomach area comes back in.

(NOW CLOSE YOUR EYES)

I can practice this by simply folding my hands over my stomach . . . then take in a deep, deep breath in through my nose . . . and now I let it out through my mouth. If my stomach pushes out when I breathe in, that's the correct breathing technique, but if mainly my chest and shoulders are moving when I breathe in, I will keep practicing until I'm breathing correctly . . .

So, as I am silent for the next few moments, I will just practice making my stomach expand out as I breathe in through my nose and have it go back in when I breathe out through my mouth. I can easily check this by watching my folded hands over my stomach.

I will practice this now, for a few minutes. I can also practice this by breathing in through my nose to the count of four, hold my breath for four seconds, and then have a big exhale out of my mouth to the count of seven.

Pause now for a few minutes and let the recorder run while you practice breathing through your diaphragm.

(CONTINUE TALKING HERE)

I know that I can easily practice this technique every night when I lie down to go to sleep by simply folding my hands and resting them on my stomach, and then practicing expanding my stomach every time I breathe in and relaxing my stomach every time I breathe out. I breathe in, expanding my stomach . . . and breathe out, relaxing my stomach. I can also practice breathing in through my nose, holding it, and exhaling through my mouth.

I now focus my concentration completely and totally on my left hand. As I focus on my left hand, I make a fist with my left hand . . . I feel the tension . . . I understand that feeling of tension . . .

And now . . . I relax my fist and notice the difference in sensations between tension and relaxation. I notice how much more comfortable and calming it is when I allow that tension to disappear and dissolve away.

Once again, I make a tight fist with my left hand . . . I feel the tension in my fist, wrist, and up my arm . . . And now, I relax my left fist . . . allowing the tension to disappear and dissolve away, allowing it to be replaced by calm, comfortable, enjoyable, relaxed muscular sensations.

Now I move the focus of concentration to my right hand, and as I do so, I make a tight fist with my right hand . . . I feel the tension in my right fist, my hand, and my arm . . . I understand that feeling . . . I allow the tension to increase tremendously . . . And now . . . I relax my right hand, completely and totally.

Again, I notice the difference in the sensations between tension and relaxation, and I notice how much more comfortable and calming it is when I allow the tension to disappear and dissolve away . . . and replace it with calm . . . comfortable . . . enjoyable . . . relaxed muscular sensations.

Once again, I make a tight fist with my right hand. I feel the tension . . . I allow that tension to build . . . And now I relax. I let the tension disappear and dissolve away . . . replacing the tension in my fist with calm, comfortable, enjoyable, relaxed muscular sensations.

Now I move the focus of my concentration to both of my arms. As I concentrate on my arms, I stretch them out in front of me as far as I can . . . I feel that tension and understand that feeling. I relax again . . . I notice the difference in sensations between tension and relaxation, and I notice how much more comfortable and calming it is when I allow the tension to disappear and be replaced by loose . . . limp . . . calm . . . comfortable muscular sensations in my arms.

Once again, I stretch my arms out in front of me. I feel the tension involved . . . I allow the tension to build . . . And now . . . I relax. The tension dissolves away and disappears and is replaced by calm . . . comfortable . . . loose . . . limp muscular sensations.

Now I move the focus of concentration to my shoulders. As I concentrate on my shoulders, I shrug them up, almost touching my ears . . . I feel that tension all the way through my shoulders, my upper back, and my neck muscles . . . And now . . . I relax.

Again, I notice the difference between the tension and the relief as I let those muscles get loose and limp . . . I feel calm, comfortable, and completely relaxed.

Once again, I shrug my shoulders up . . . I feel the tension in my upper back, as I am forcing my shoulders up toward my ears . . . And now . . . I relax. All the tension that was there is disappearing and dissolving away, and it is being replaced with calm . . . comfortable . . . enjoyable . . . relaxed . . . muscular sensations.

Now I move the focus of my concentration to my forehead and scalp. As I think about my forehead and scalp, keeping my eyes closed, I raise my eyebrows as high as I can and feel the creases across my forehead and scalp . . . And now, I relax my forehead and scalp muscles. I notice the wonderful sensations as I allow my forehead and scalp to smooth out and feel calm . . . comfortable . . . and completely relaxed.

Again, I raise my eyebrows, causing creases across my forehead and scalp . . . And now I relax. All of the tension that was there disappears and dissolves away and is replaced by calm . . . comfortable . . . enjoyable . . . relaxed . . . smooth . . . muscular sensations.

(NOTE: If you are wearing contact lenses, skip the next section on relaxing your eye muscles.)

Now I concentrate on my eyes. As I concentrate on my eyes, I close them as tightly as I can. I feel that tension . . . I understand that feeling . . . And now, I relax my eye muscles . . . allowing that tension to disappear and dissolve away . . . replacing it with calm . . . comfortable . . . enjoyable . . . relaxed . . . muscular sensations.

Once again, I close my eyes tightly . . . I feel the tension . . . And now, I relax. All of the tension disappears and dissolves away and is replaced by calm . . . comfortable . . . enjoyable . . . relaxed . . . muscular sensations.

Now I focus my concentration on my neck . . . As I concentrate on my neck, I turn my head to the left as far as I can . . . And now I turn to the right . . . now down into my chest . . . And now, I relax ... All of the muscles of my neck are getting loose and limp . . . They're feeling calm, comfortable . . . and completely relaxed.

Once again, I turn my head to the left . . . and now to the right . . . now down into my chest . . . and relax . . . I feel complete and total relaxation . . . almost as if the muscles of my neck are like ropes that have been tied in knots, and these knots are now unraveling and leaving loose . . . limp . . . calm . . . comfortable muscular sensations. Loose . . . limp . . . calm . . . comfortable . . . muscular sensations.

Now I focus on my breathing. I imagine that I'm inside my body, listening to my breathing. I listen to how deeply I breathe . . . I listen to how rapidly or slowly I breathe . . . I notice that as I take slower, deeper breaths, it's much more relaxing and calming. As I take slower . . . deeper breaths . . . it's much more relaxing and calming.

Now I take a nice deep breath in through my nose and hold it, just holding the tension . . . letting it all gather in my lungs . . . And now I exhale through my mouth. All of the tension is leaving my body . . . completely and totally. Once again, I take a nice . . . deep breath . . . I feel the tension . . . and exhale all of that tension away, leaving in its place calm . . . comfortable . . . relaxed . . . muscular sensations. Calm . . . comfortable . . . relaxed . . . muscular sensations.

I know that every time I want to relax deeply, I can give myself a series of slow, deep breaths . . . in through my nose to the count of four . . . hold it to the count of four . . . let the tension build . . . and then exhale, pushing it out forcefully from my mouth, to the count of seven. I breathe in . . . hold it . . . and now breathe out through my mouth . . . allowing all of the tension to dissolve away . . . completely and totally. As I breathe in . . . through my nose . . . and out through my mouth . . . I feel the relaxation getting deeper and deeper. Every time I breathe in . . . through my nose . . . and out through my mouth . . . I feel the relaxation growing . . . deeper and deeper.

Now I move the focus of concentration to my stomach. As I focus on my stomach, I pull my stomach muscles in as far as I can. Now I relax my stomach muscles . . . I let the tension disappear and dissolve away, and I allow my stomach muscles to get completely and totally relaxed . . . Once again, I pull my stomach muscles in, feel the tension . . . and relax. All of the tension in my stomach muscles disappears and dissolves away . . . being replaced by calm, comfortable, relaxed, loose, limp muscular sensations . . .

Still focusing on my stomach, I do the opposite. I push my stomach muscles out . . . And I feel that tension . . . Now, I relax. I notice the difference . . . I notice how much more comfortable and calming it feels to just let go. Once again, I push my stomach muscles out . . . I feel the tension . . . And now . . . I relax all of those muscles . . . calm, comfortable, relaxed muscular sensations . . .

Now I focus on my buttocks and my thighs. I squeeze my buttocks and thigh muscles, and I feel the tension in the lower part of my body . . . Now, I relax . . . Once again, I squeeze my buttocks and thigh muscles . . . and then I relax. All of the tension in my lower body is dissolving away and disappearing and being replaced by calm . . . comfortable . . . relaxed . . . muscular sensations . . .

Now I concentrate on my legs and feet. I stretch my legs and feet out, pointing my toes away from me and stretching my feet out as far as I can. I feel that tension and notice how that feels . . . And now, I relax. I dissolve away that tension completely and totally . . . replacing it with loose . . . limp . . . calm . . . comfortable . . . relaxed muscular sensations. Loose . . . limp . . . calm . . . comfortable . . . muscular sensations. Such a good feeling in my legs and feet . . . such a relaxing feeling . . .

Once again, I stretch my legs and feet out, pointing my toes away from me . . . I feel that tension and notice how that feels. And now, I relax. I dissolve away that tension completely and totally . . . replacing it with loose . . . limp . . . calm . . . comfortable . . . relaxed muscular sensations.

I continue my slow, deep, relaxing breathing, and I tell myself that with each deep breath I take in through my nose and exhale out through my mouth, I feel relaxation spreading from my scalp down my face across my eyes . . . past the bridge of my nose . . . across my mouth . . . down into my neck . . . and across my shoulders . . . all the way down my arms to my wrists and to my fingers . . . down through my chest, stomach, and abdomen . . . down my back . . . to my lower trunk . . . down through my thighs to my knees . . . legs . . . ankles . . . feet . . . and toes.

As I continue to relax . . . deeper and deeper . . . I clear away all worries, concerns, and distractions . . .

That's right . . . And I can stay in this relaxed state as long as I wish . . .

I know that my mind may drift off to a relaxing memory, a peaceful and serene place that I have visited in the past. Perhaps I will remember a wonderful and calming experience I had sometime in my childhood . . . perhaps a favorite family vacation or a special place my friends and I used to go to . . . perhaps in the woods or a tree hut . . . or at the beach . . . or in the snow. It doesn't really matter what memory comes to mind. What does matter is that I just allow my mind to drift as I listen to my own soothing voice describing this place . . .

(Now just describe into the recorder the scene that comes to mind . . . The place, the season, the time of day, where you are, who—if anyone—is with you, what you are doing, the weather, the aromas, the colors, the breeze, what you hear and see, and all details you can recall.)

Perhaps I can already feel relaxed, comfortable sensations entering my shoulder or a leg or an arm as I listen to my voice describing this favorite scene. Perhaps I can briefly focus on any sounds that may be around me, in this room, at this very moment . . . like a ticking clock or the distant murmur of traffic . . .

Although I may hear these sounds occasionally as I focus on my voice, they only serve to lull me into an even deeper state of relaxation and comfort.

I wonder if I can recall other experiences of drifting off. Perhaps being so completely engrossed in a movie or TV show that I lost track of everyone in the room . . . lost track of all the sounds made by these people, and perhaps I only paid attention to those sounds once the show ended. Perhaps a favorite song comes to mind from my past, bringing me another memory that is soothing and comforting, and perhaps the music is in the background now as I listen to my voice drifting deeper and deeper.

Peaceful and quiet feelings flow through me right now . . . so relaxed and peaceful. Perhaps the music lingers in the background, and my conscious mind is drifting off to another place . . . another time. There is no need for me to try to make this happen . . .

It just happens. Although there is certainly no need to understand how these wonderful feelings develop or why they develop, I just flow with it . . . absorb it. Perhaps I notice my breathing, and how it changes to slow . . . deep . . . breathing. I know that deep relaxation can take many forms . . . from heavy feelings, to light, floating feelings, and to warm or tingly sensations. It doesn't matter which I feel . . .

They all represent relaxation.

I don't know if my mind will begin by relaxing just one of my fingers, or perhaps it will choose a shoulder or a leg to begin with. My mind can focus on the parts of my body that are beginning to relax, or it can drift off to another place . . . It's up to me. My mind will continue the process of relaxing my entire body, perhaps randomly, perhaps in a pattern beginning with the top of my head making its way all the way down to the tips of my toes. With every word I say, I'm feeling the relaxation flowing deeper and deeper throughout my body.

(Pause here for a minute or two, letting the recorder continue to record the silence.)

(CONTINUE HERE IN A LOUDER VOICE)

It is now time to come back across time and space, to here and now. I shall count from one to five, and as I do so, I will come back to here and now, awake and alert. **One** . . . **two** . . . coming back across time and space . . . **three** . . . stretching my muscles now . . . becoming fully alert and awake but remaining relaxed, confident, and excited about my ability to relax myself on command . . . **four** . . . free from old scripts and fears and knowing that every single time I listen to this recording, I will get more and more relaxed . . . stronger and stronger, more and more self-assured, able to deal with any challenges that come along . . . and **five** . . . fully awake, alert, fully refreshed. I open my eyes now, fully awake, refreshed, and alert.

About the Author

Dr. Jack Singer is a professional psychologist who practices the specialties of Clinical, Sport, and Industrial/Organizational Psychology. He regularly consults with CEOs, financial advisors, and sales teams, teaching all of his clients the same skills he teaches to elite athletes. Dr. Jack is also a professional speaker and trainer who has conducted training programs for financial professionals and insurance producers across the U.S. and Australia, as well as for Fortune 1000 companies from Miami to Malaysia. Jack has been awarded diplomate status from the American Academy of Behavioral Medicine and the Psychology Division of the National Institute of Sport Professionals, and he has taught in the psychology departments of seven universities, including an assistant professorship at the U.S. Air Force Academy.

The wide variety of his experience and services ranges from designing keynote presentations and team-building re-TREATS for financial professionals and producer-incentive programs ... to providing advisor coaching and client appreciation events ... to training world-class, Olympic, and professional athletes. Jack is renowned across the United States for his innovative work in stress mastery, both in personal lives and in the busy workplace.

A sought-after media guest, Jack is called on frequently to comment on CNN, MSNBC, The Glenn Beck Program, Fox Sports, and ESPN, as well as talk radio shows throughout the United States, Canada, and Australia. He has published more than 175 articles in financial, business, sales, human resources, psychological, medical, and sports periodicals, and his consulting work has been featured in *USA Today*.

Jack has authored *The Teacher's Ultimate Stress Mastery Guide*, as well as co-authored two books, his latest being *Dynamic Health*. Dr. Jack has also produced several self-help programs, including hypnotic audios for raising self-esteem and mastering anger, and for athletes to maintain consistent, peak performance.

As a professional speaker, Dr. Jack has enjoyed wide acclaim for his powerful and funny keynote presentations, including **"Developing & Maintaining the Mindset of a Champion Financial Advisor," "Powerful Prescriptions to Prevent Hardening of the Attitudes," "All Stressed Up ... and Nowhere to Go,"** and **"How to Live Much Longer Than Your Kids Hoped You Would!"**

All of Dr. Jack's keynotes are customized specifically for the goals and needs of his audiences, and he is committed to helping everyone he trains "add years to their lives, while they add life to their years."

"Dr. Jack has couch ... will travel."

For more information regarding his consulting and professional speaking services:

Visit his website at
www.developthemindsetofachampion.com

Contact him at 1–800–497–9880

E-mail him at drjack@funspeaker.com

www.ingramcontent.com/pod-product-compliance
Lightning Source LLC
Chambersburg PA
CBHW060511300426
44112CB00017B/2620